Communications in Computer and Information Science 1324

More information about this series at http://www.springer.com/series/7899

Ulf Brefeld · Jesse Davis · Jan Van Haaren ·
Albrecht Zimmermann (Eds.)

Machine Learning and Data Mining for Sports Analytics

7th International Workshop, MLSA 2020
Co-located with ECML/PKDD 2020
Ghent, Belgium, September 14–18, 2020
Proceedings

 Springer

Editors
Ulf Brefeld
Leuphana University of Lüneburg
Lüneburg, Germany

Jan Van Haaren
SciSports
Amersfoort, The Netherlands

Jesse Davis ⓘ
Katholieke Universiteit Leuven
Leuven, Belgium

Albrecht Zimmermann ⓘ
Université de Caen Normandie
Caen, France

ISSN 1865-0929   ISSN 1865-0937 (electronic)
Communications in Computer and Information Science
ISBN 978-3-030-64911-1   ISBN 978-3-030-64912-8 (eBook)
https://doi.org/10.1007/978-3-030-64912-8

This Springer imprint is published by the registered company Springer Nature Switzerland AG
The registered company address is: Gewerbestrasse 11, 6330 Cham, Switzerland

Preface

The Machine Learning and Data Mining for Sports Analytics (MLSA) workshop aims to bring people from outside of the Machine Learning and Data Mining community into contact with researchers from that community who are working on Sports Analytics. The 7th edition of the workshop was co-located with the European Conference on Machine Learning and Principles and Practice of Knowledge Discovery (ECML PKDD 2020).

Sports Analytics has been a steadily growing and rapidly evolving area over the last decade, both in US professional sports leagues and in European football leagues. The recent implementation of strict financial fair-play regulations in European football will definitely increase the importance of Sports Analytics in the coming years. In addition, there is the popularity of sports betting. The developed techniques are being used for decision support in all aspects of professional sports, including but not limited to:

- Match strategy, tactics, and analysis
- Player acquisition, player valuation, and team spending
- Training regimens and focus
- Injury prediction and prevention
- Performance management and prediction
- Match outcome and league table prediction
- Tournament design and scheduling
- Betting odds calculation

The interest in the topic has grown so much that there is now an annual conference on Sports Analytics at the MIT Sloan School of Management, which has been attended by representatives from over 70 professional sports teams in eminent leagues such as the Major League Baseball, National Basketball Association, National Football League, National Hockey League, Major League Soccer, English Premier League, and the German Bundesliga. Furthermore, sports data providers such as Statsbomb and Opta have started making performance data publicly available to stimulate researchers who have the skills and vision to make a difference in the sports analytics community. Moreover, the National Football league has been sponsoring a Big Data Bowl where they release data and a concrete question to try to engage the analytics community.

There has been growing interest in the Machine Learning and Data Mining community about this topic, and the 2020 edition of MLSA built on the success of prior editions at ECML PKDD 2013, ECML PKDD 2015 – ECML/PKDD 2019.

In 2020, the workshop received 22 submissions of which 13 were selected after a single-blind reviewing process involving at least 3 Program Committee members per paper. Of these papers, 3 were extended abstracts and are therefore not included in the post-proceedings. The contributions covered a wide range of sports, including the ever-popular soccer but also climbing, cricket, cycling, ice hockey, and long-distance running. Topics included tactical analysis, outcome predictions, data acquisition, performance optimization, and player evaluation.

The workshop featured an invited presentation by David Sumpter from University of Uppsala, Sweden, on "Using collective motion models to help players improve their game."

Further information about the workshop can be found on the workshop's website at https://dtai.cs.kuleuven.be/events/MLSA20/.

October 2020

Ulf Brefeld
Jesse Davis
Jan Van Haaren
Albrecht Zimmermann

Organization

Workshop Co-chairs

Ulf Brefeld	Leuphana University, Germany
Jesse Davis	KU Leuven, Belgium
Jan Van Haaren	SciSports, The Netherlands
Albrecht Zimmermann	Université de Caen, France

Program Committee

Max Adema	SciSports, The Netherlands
Gennady Andrienko	Fraunhofer, Germany
Harish S. Bhat	University of California, Merced, USA
Matthew van Bommel	Sacramento Kings, USA
Arne De Brabandere	KU Leuven, Belgium
Lotte Bransen	SciSports, The Netherlands
Paolo Cintia	University of Pisa, Italy
Tom Decroos	KU Leuven, Belgium
Kurt Driessens	Maastricht University, The Netherlands
Martin Eastwood	www.pena.lt/y, UK
Javier Fernandez	FC Barcelona, Spain
Clément Gautrais	KU Leuven, Belgium
Mehdi Kaytoue	Infologic, France
Patrick Lambrix	Linköping University, Sweden
Jan Lasek	Systems Research Institute, Polish Academy of Sciences, Poland
Arie-Willem de Leeuw	Universiteit Leiden, The Netherlands
Christophe Ley	Ghent University, Belgium
Laurentius Meerhoff	Leiden Institute of Advanced Computer Science, The Netherlands
Wannes Meert	KU Leuven, Belgium
Tim Op De Beéck	KU Leuven, Belgium
Luca Pappalardo	University of Pisa, Italy
Konstantinos Pelechrinis	University of Pittsburgh, USA
François Rioult	Université de Caen, France
Pieter Robberechts	KU Leuven, Belgium
Oliver Schulte	Simon Fraser University, France
Jan Van Haaren	SciSports, The Netherlands
Guillermo Vinue	University of Valencia, Spain

Contents

Football

Routine Inspection: A Playbook for Corner Kicks

Laurie Shaw[1(✉)] and Sudarshan Gopaladesikan[2]

[1] Harvard University, Cambridge, USA
`laurie.shaw@cfa.harvard.edu`
[2] Benfica SL, Lisbon, Portugal
`sgopaladesikan@slbenfica.pt`

Abstract. We present a set of tools for identifying and studying the offensive and defensive strategies used by football teams in corner kick situations: their corner playbooks. Drawing from methods in topic modelling, our tools classify corners based on the runs made by the attacking players, enabling us to identify the distinct corner routines used by individual teams and search tracking data to find corners that exhibit specific features of interest. We use a supervised machine learning approach to identify whether individual defenders are marking man-to-man or zonally and study the positioning of zonal defenders over many matches. We demonstrate how our methods can be used for opposition analysis by highlighting the offensive and defensive corner strategies used by teams in our data over the course of a season.

1 Introduction

A cross from the winger is blocked by a defender, who concedes a corner. The crowd roars, anticipating a goal-scoring opportunity. The statistics, however, predict a different outcome. According to data collected by OPTA, in the 2019–20 season of the Portuguese Primeira Liga, just 45 goals have been scored from 3082 corners – a 1.5% conversion rate. In the German Bundesliga the conversion rate was 1.9%, and in Spain's La Liga it was only 0.8%. Similarly, Power et al. (2018) found that only 2.1% of corners resulted in a goal over three seasons of the English Premier League. Given that corner kicks are one of the few attacking situations that occur in nearly every match – and that they can easily be rehearsed in training – the low average conversion rate is somewhat surprising. Indeed, some teams have been able to achieve a much higher success rate [1].

Previous work has focused on studying general measures of corner strategy, such as delivery type (inswinging, outswinging or straight), the ball delivery zone (e.g. near post, far post, center), the number of attacking players involved and whether they were 'static' or 'dynamic' [1–5]. Casal et al. (2015) analyzed the factors that lead to a shot or a goal, finding that match time, the number of intervening attackers, and whether the attack was 'dynamic' were the most significant variables. Power et al. (2018) found that a goal was more likely to be

© Springer Nature Switzerland AG 2020
U. Brefeld et al. (Eds.): MLSA 2020, CCIS 1324, pp. 3–16, 2020.
https://doi.org/10.1007/978-3-030-64912-8_1

scored on the second ball (i.e. after a touch from a teammate) than directly from the corner kick. From a defensive perspective, they found that hybrid systems concede the most dangerous shots relative to pure zonal or man-to-man systems.

With the advent of player tracking data, it is now possible to perform a detailed analysis of the synchronised runs made by the attacking players – the rehearsed *routines* that define the core of offensive corner tactics. Tools developed for this purpose would enable analysts to identify and study the corner routines used frequently by an opponent over a large number of matches. Furthermore, while previous studies of corner defence have focused on general classifications of the defensive system (zonal, man marking or hybrid), it is quite rare for teams to employ a purely zonal or man-marking system: most use some form of a hybrid system [1]. The challenge is to identify which defenders are man-marking, which defenders have been assigned to zones and where those zones are located.

This paper aims to meet these challenges. Using a combination of statistical and machine learning techniques and a large sample of tracking data, we have developed tools to classify corner routines based on the runs made by the attacking players, enabling us to identify the distinct corner routines employed by teams in our data. We have trained a supervised learning algorithm to identify whether *individual defenders* have been assigned a man-marking or zonal role and studied the positioning of the zonal players of teams in our sample.

The paper is organised as follows. In Sect. 2 we describe our data and the selection of our corner sample. In Sect. 3 we describe our technique for classifying corner routines based on the runs made by individual players. In Sect. 4 we describe our methodology for identifying the roles of the defending players during corner kicks, making use of a unique training set provided by the analysts at SL Benfica. In Sect. 5 we demonstrate how our methods can be used for opposition analysis, before concluding in Sect. 6.

2 Data

Our analysis uses tracking and event data for 234 matches from a single season of an elite professional league. The tracking data for each match consists of the positions of all 22 players and the ball, sampled at a frequency 25 Hz. Individual player identities are tagged in the data, enabling tracking of each player over time. The event data consists of a log of each on-ball event that took place during a match (e.g. passes, shots, tackles and interceptions), including the identity of the players involved and the time and location on the pitch at which the event occurred.

We use the event data to provide an initial estimate for the time at which each corner kick was taken during a match. To identify the exact frame we use a combination of factors, including the acceleration of the ball and a *ball in play* flag included in the tracking data. After removing short corners (which are not included in this analysis) and a small number of corners for which ball tracking errors were identified, we were left with a sample of 1723 corner kicks. Finally, to aid comparisons, we reflected the positions of players and the ball so that corners always appear to be taken from the left side of the pitch.

3   Classifying Corner Routines

Figure 1 illustrates two examples of corner routines in our sample. The offensive strategies are clearly very different: the starting positions of the players, their trajectories and the delivery target of the ball. One of the main goals of this work is to develop tools to search tracking data to identify the different corner routines used by teams over many matches. We achieve this by developing a classification system for describing the main features of a routine based on the runs made by the individual players in the attacking team. This system enables us to find corners that have similar features, or to quickly search the data for corners that exhibit a particular feature of interest.

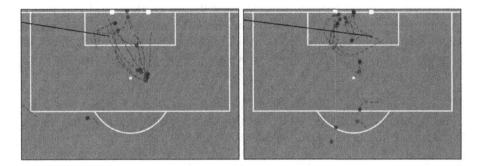

Fig. 1. Two corners in our data depicting very different offensive strategies. The red (blue) markers indicate the positions of the attacking (defending) players two seconds before the corner is taken. The dashed lines indicate each player's trajectory, from two seconds before the corner was taken until approximately two seconds after. The solid black line indicates the path of the ball over the same time period. (Color figure online)

Our methodology has two key steps:

1. a data-defined zonal system for classifying player runs based on their start and target locations; and
2. a topic model for identifying player runs that frequently co-occur in corner routines.

We now summarize each of these steps in more detail. Note that the trajectory of the ball does not feature in our system. This is because the ball does not always reach the intended target, either because it was intercepted or because the cross was not sufficiently accurate. We recognize that the ball can also be delivered using different trajectory types: curving away from goal, curving towards goal, floated or flat. We intend to incorporate this information in a follow-up study evaluating the effectiveness of different corner routines.

3.1   Classifying Player Runs

The basic building blocks of a corner routine are the individual runs made by the players. We define a run entirely in terms of the initial and target location; we do not attempt to model a player's trajectory between those locations. Initial positions are measured exactly two seconds before the corner is taken – this corresponds to the moment at which the average speed of players typically starts to increase as they begin their runs. The target locations are defined as being either the positions of the players exactly one second after the first on-ball event following the corner, or two seconds after the corner is taken, whichever occurs first[1]. It is impossible to know the true intended target location of a player, we simply assume that attacking players always reach their target.

We allocate players to pairs of zones based on their initial and target locations. These zones are defined using the distribution of the initial and target positions of all the attacking players in our sample of corners. The process starts with the distribution of the target positions. The upper panel of Fig. 2 indicates the target positions of nearly 15000 attacking players measured over the 1723 corners in our sample (only players in the attacking quarter of the field are plotted). The cloud of points in the top-left corner corresponds to the positions of the corner takers shortly after each corner is taken.

Target zones are defined by fitting a 15-component Gaussian Mixture Model (GMM) using the expectation-maximisation algorithm [6,7]. We find that 15 components (that is, 15 bivariate normal distributions) are sufficient and that adding further components does not result in a significant improvement in the log-likelihood. The lower-left panel of Fig. 2 shows each of the 15 components in the GMM. The seven components of the model located in the penalty area are indicated by blue ellipses and labelled a to g. We henceforth refer to these as the *active zones*. Individual points belonging to the same active zone are coloured accordingly. Players with a target position near one of these seven active zones are assumed to be directly involved in the corner routine: these are referred to as *active players*. Players that do not end near an active zone are ignored in our analysis.

The upper-right panel of Fig. 2 shows the initial positions of attacking players, two seconds before the corner is taken. Active players are coloured blue and form two groups: those that start inside the six yard box, and the players that are initially clustered around, and depicted slightly to the right of, the penalty spot. Points coloured black are players that were not actively involved in the corner (including the corner taker, who is no longer involved after taking the corner). To define the initial zones of active players we fit a 6 component GMM model (with some outlier removal) to their initial positions. The six components of our fit are labelled 1 to 6 in the lower-right panel of Fig. 2. The fit was not improved significantly by adding additional components to the model.

Allocating players to initial and target zones enables a simple encoding of player runs. Active players are allocated to an initial zone (1–6) and a target

---

[1] Measuring positions one second after the first ball event helps to identify the target position of players aiming to reach a flick-on.

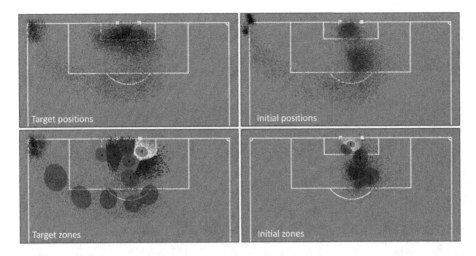

Fig. 2. (*upper left*) The target positions of all 15000 attacking players in our sample of corners. (*lower left*) The results of the 15-component GMM fit to the target positions. The seven 'active zones' in the penalty area are represented by blue ellipses and labelled *a-g*. Individual points are coloured according to the active zone to which they belong. (*upper right*) The initial positions of all 15000 attacking players. Players coloured blue are tagged as 'active'. (*lower panel*) The results of a 6-component GMM fit to the initial positions of the active players.

zone (a-g) based on their initial and target positions. For example, in the left panel of Fig. 1 the four attacking players that start their runs next to the penalty spot are initially in zone *4* and move into target zones *b*, *c* and *d*. Their runs are therefore encoded as {*4b,4b,4c,4d*}.

3.2   Topic Modelling

The runs made by the attacking players are coordinated and synchronised: some players will attempt to draw away defenders, while others will attempt to intercept the ball. The second step of our method is to identify the types of runs that are frequently combined in corner routines. To achieve this, we draw inspiration from topic modelling by making the analogy between runs and words, combinations of runs and topics, and corner kicks and documents.

We use non-negative matrix factorization (NMF) to represent the corners in our data in terms of a basis set of run combinations. NMF decomposes an initial matrix, called the *term matrix*, into two lower-rank, non-negative matrices, W and H [8,9]. Our term matrix has the following dimensions: 42 rows by 1723 columns. The rows represent all 42 combinations of the 6 initial and 7 target zones and each column corresponds to a corner in our data set. Each element in the term matrix is given by the sum of the probabilities that each active player in the corner made a run between a specific pair of initial and target zones. For each player, this is calculated by multiplying the GMM posterior probability that the player started in the initial zone by the probability that he ended in the target zone. W represents the run combinations (or topics) that frequently co-occur in the data; H tells you how to construct each corner in the data from the run combinations.

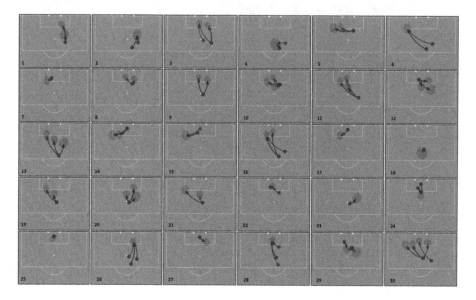

Fig. 3. The thirty features, or frequently co-occurring runs, identified by our topic model.

We find that the corners in our data can be accurately reconstructed from a set of 30 run combinations (henceforth referred to as *features*). These features are shown in Fig. 3. In some cases, a feature consists of just a single run – this is because the same run may occur in many different corner routines. We can represent every corner in our data in terms of a sub-sample of these features and group together corners that exhibit similar features to identify distinct routines. For example, the corner depicted in the left panel of Fig. 1 exhibits features 9 and 19, which describe the runs from the penalty spot towards the near post, goal center and far post. The corner depicted in the right panel of Fig. 1 strongly exhibits feature 12, which describes runs from the near post towards the far post. Both corners also exhibit feature 25: an attacking player standing close to where the goalkeeper would be located.

We can also use the feature representation to rapidly search large numbers of matches to find corners that exhibit a certain feature of interest, or a combination of features. Figure 4 shows other corners in our sample that strongly exhibit feature 12. Three teams in particular make frequent use of this corner routine.

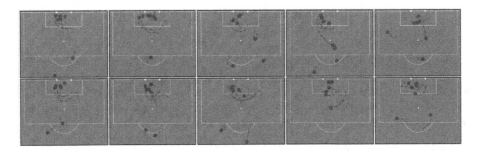

Fig. 4. Ten corners in our sample that strongly exhibit feature 12 – runs from the near post round to the far post. Only attacking team players are shown. Large dots indicate the initial positions of each player and dashed lines show their trajectories.

4   Identifying Defensive Roles

The defining feature of defensive strategy in corner kick situations is the use of man- or zonal-marking systems. Man-to-man marking requires a player to closely track a specific opponent, while zonal marking requires a player to defend a spatial region (we consider defending a goal post as zonal marking). Few teams use an exclusively zonal marking system and it is rare for a team to have no zonal marking players whatsoever. For example, Power et al. (2018) find that 80% of the teams in their data employed hybrid systems (i.e., a mixture of man-to-man and zonal marking).

For this reason we work on the level of individual players, using supervised machine learning to classify the role of each defender in the penalty area. We use the popular XGBoost implementation of gradient boosted decision trees [10] to calculate the probability that each defender in the penalty area is marking man-to-man. Gradient boosted decision trees have been shown to be a powerful tool for solving classification problems in an efficient manner [11].

The key distinction between man-to-man and zonal marking is that, in the former, a player is marking a moving target rather than a static region. Treating attackers near the goalkeeper as a special case and emphasizing the locomotive reaction of the defenders, we selected the metrics listed below as predictive variables. These variables were vetted by video analysts at SL Benfica[2]:

1. initial position (x coordinate)*
2. initial position (y coordinate)*
3. distance between start and target positions*
4. initial proximity to goalkeeper*
5. average distance travelled by attacking players in the same initial zone*
6. average distance travelled by other defenders in the same initial zone*
7. initial zone
8. target zone

---

[2] Our methodology does not identify the specific opponent a defender is man-marking.

9. # of attacking players in the same initial zone
10. # of other defenders in the same initial zone

To provide data for training and testing, analysts at SL Benfica watched a sample of 500 movies of corners selected from our data set and manually identified the jersey numbers of the man-to-man and zonal defenders. In total, 3907 defenders were evaluated: 55% were tagged as marking man-to-man and the remainder tagged as zonal; the two classes are therefore well-balanced. Figure 5 shows the initial positions of zonal (upper-left) and man-marking players (upper-right) in the analysts' sample. It is clearly evident that player positions are a strong discriminator.

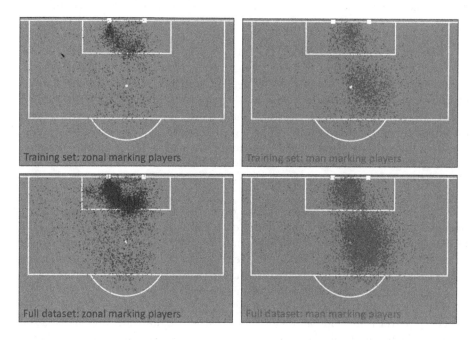

Fig. 5. (*upper*) The initial positions of zonal (left) and man-marking players (right) based on the manual classifications made by Benfica's analysts. (*lower*) Results for the full sample, based on the classifications predicted by the trained XGboost model.

We use 66% of the analysts' annotated sample as the training set, with the remaining 33% reserved as a test set to evaluate the performance of the model. We obtain a classification accuracy of 83.5%; training instead with 10-fold cross validation results in a classification accuracy of $83.4\% \pm 2.1\%$. The most predictive features, selected via their F-score, are marked with an asterisk in the list above. We apply the decision tree to our remaining sample of 1223 corners to predict the roles of each defending player. The initial positions of players classified as zonal (lower-left) and man-marking (lower-right) are shown in Fig. 5.

There is clearly a strong resemblance to the analyst-annotated sample. Note that the spatial distribution of man-marking defenders also resembles the initial positions of the active attacking players shown in Fig. 2.

5   Applications: Opposition Analysis

Anticipating how an opponent will play in different phases of a game is a crucial aspect of pre-match preparation [12,13]. However, evaluating an opponent using video is a time-consuming process and so club analysts are often limited to studying approximately five matches to inform their reports for the coaching staff. Such a small sample of matches provides only a limited insight into the range of set-piece strategies that might be utilized by the opponent.

Our methodology enables us to rapidly identify the key features of the corner strategies used by teams over a large sample of their matches. In this section we demonstrate its application to opposition analysis, highlighting the corner routines used frequently by teams in our sample over the course of a season and analysing the systems they employed to defend corners.

5.1   Offensive Strategy

Figure 6 shows four corner routines used regularly by teams A (red), B (blue), C (green) and D (black) in our data set. Each panel shows a specific example of a routine that the team used multiple times throughout the season. Distinct routines were identified by clustering corners based on their feature activation (columns of the H matrix). The circles indicate the starting position of each player and the dashed lines indicate their runs in the few seconds that follow the corner kick. The black dotted line indicates the trajectory of the ball. All corners are translated so that the ball is delivered from the left corner of the pitch.

It is clear that our methodology has identified a set of distinct routines for each team. A popular strategy used by almost every team in our sample is the *jellyfish*. In this strategy, three or four players start in a cluster outside the six-yard box before making gradually diverging runs towards the box (see rows 3 and 4 in Fig. 6). Closer inspection reveals that teams employ different versions of this strategy, varying the position of the initial cluster and the length of run made by each player. One example is the *love train* – in which players start in a line, rather than a cluster – as popularised by the England team at the 2018 World Cup. Team B regularly employed the *love train*, with the line starting near the penalty spot (third row). They also used a variation of the *jellyfish* in which the players started in the far corner of the penalty area (fourth row). Team A employed a variation in which a player makes a run around and behind the initial cluster, aiming for the far post (fourth row) and an unusual routine in which four players start at the far edge of the six-yard box before running horizontally towards the ball (second row).

Team A	Team B	Team C	Team D

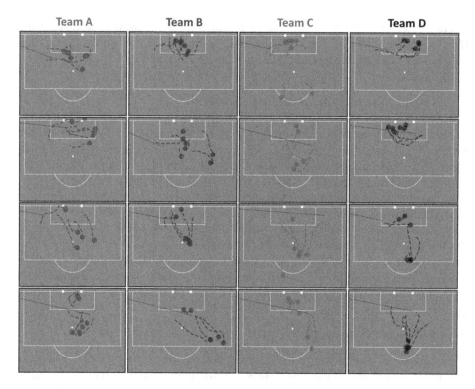

Fig. 6. Examples of popular corner routines employed by four teams in our dataset. (Color figure online)

Another class of routines is the six-yard box *overload*, in which four or five attacking players initially crowd the six-yard box. Figure 6 shows some distinct variations: the second row of Team D shows a routine in which two players positioned in front of the near post circle out of the six-yard box and round towards the far post to intercept a deep delivery. The first row shows the reverse of this: two players at the far post run around the box to intercept a near post delivery. Team B also regularly employed variants of the *overload* (e.g. first row).

The teams in our data did not alternate randomly from one routine to another as they took corners. Rather, they would typically use a routine regularly over a series of consecutive matches and then discard it, perhaps reintroducing the routine later in the season. For example, Team C attempted the corner depicted in the fourth row five times over three consecutive games, discarded it for six games and then used it three times in one game. This emphasizes the need to scan over a large number of matches to fully scout the range of offensive strategies that might be employed by an opponent in their next match.

5.2   Defence

The objective of offensive corner routines is to disrupt the defensive structure of their opponents and create sufficient space for the target player to have a clear shot on goal. The fundamental question for the attacking team is therefore: *what is our opponent's strategy for defending corner kicks?* Fig. 7 shows the total number of players allocated to zonal or man-marking roles for four teams in our sample during their first 30 matches of the season (the teams depicted are not the same set of teams discussed in the previous section). Red indicates the number of players in zonal marking roles, blue indicates the number of players in man-marking roles. The large dots connected by lines show the median number of players in either role over all the corners defended in each match; the small pale dots show the numbers in either role for the individual corners in each match.

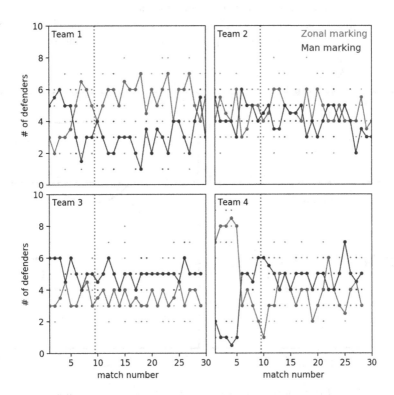

Fig. 7. The number of man-marking and zonally marking defenders over the first 30 matches for four teams in our dataset. Red (blue) lines indicate the median number of zonal (man-marking) defenders over the corners in each match. The small points indicate the numbers for the individual corners. Matches to the left of the dashed lines were included in the analyst-annotated sample. (Color figure online)

Team 1 defended with a predominantly zonal system, supplemented by two or three man-marking players. Team 2 adopted an almost perfectly hybrid system with similar numbers of man-marking and zonal defenders, while Team 3 consistently defended with more players in man-marking roles. Team 4 changed their defensive system during the season. In their first five matches they used a predominantly zonal system, with eight outfield players assigned to zones and typically just one player man-marking. In game six they made a wholesale change to their defensive strategy, significantly increasing the number of man-marking defenders and halving the number of players assigned to zonal roles. The motivations behind the change seem evident: in the first five matches they conceded 2 goals from 32 corners, including 1 from 2 during game five. Following the change, the rate at which they conceded goals from corners halved to 4 goals in 120 corners.

Having identified the players allocated to a zonal role, we can investigate where the zones were located. Figure 8 presents heat-maps for the spatial distribution of the zonal defenders for Teams 1–4 over the 30 matches. A darker shade of blue indicates a higher occupation rate for a given location.

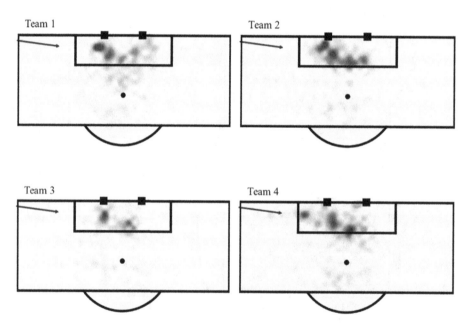

Fig. 8. The spatial distribution of zonal marking defenders for Teams 1–4 in Fig. 7 over their 30 matches. The red shading for Team 4 indicates the distribution of zonal defenders over their first 5 matches, the blue shading for their remaining 25 matches. The arrow indicates the direction from which the corner is taken. (Color figure online)

Team 1 used a predominantly zonal system and this is reflected in spatial distribution of their zonal players. There are four clearly distinct peaks in the distribution forming a circle around the goalmouth, the most prominent being in front of the near post. There is a fainter fifth peak next to the far post, suggesting a zonal defender was sometimes positioned there, and a cloud between the six-yard box and the penalty spot where the remaining zonal players were positioned (although not necessarily in the same place in every corner). A similar pattern is observed for Team 2, albeit with no defender at the far post and fewer zonal players outside the 6-yard box. Team 3 is a predominantly man-marking team, and there were only two areas routinely defended by a zonal player: next to the front post and at the edge of the six-yard box.

Team 4 is an interesting case. The red regions indicate the distribution of zonal players in their first five games, during which they employed a predominantly zonal marking system. There is insufficient data to identify exactly where each player was stationed, but they were clearly distributed broadly throughout the 6-yard box (and players guarding either post are also visible). After the tactical change in game 6, Team 4 typically retained at least three zonal players, with one player being positioned significantly in advance of the near post.

6   Conclusion

Using a season's worth of player tracking and event data, we have conducted an in-depth analysis of the offensive and defensive strategies employed by teams in corner kick situations. By studying and classifying the runs made by the attacking team, we have created a system for describing corners that enables us to characterise a corner routine in terms of the run combinations made by the attacking players. This allows us to search a large sample of corners to find certain characteristics (e.g. a particular run, or combinations of runs) or group similar corner routines.

We have also presented a supervised learning model for classifying the role of each defending player in corner situations. Using a sample of 500 corners manually annotated by club analysts, we trained the XGBoost algorithm to predict whether each defending player was instructed to man-mark or zonally mark, obtaining a cross-validated classification accuracy of $83.4 \pm 2.1\%$. The main predictors of player role are their initial positions, distance travelled during the corner, proximity to the goalkeeper, and the average distance travelled by nearby teammates and opponents.

We have demonstrated how these tools can be applied to provide unprecedented insights into the strategies used by teams in corner kick situations, identifying the distinct corner routines employed by four teams over the course of a season. Our methodology for identifying the defensive roles of individual players will also help analysts and coaches to find vulnerabilities in the defensive systems of their opponents and exploit them.

A natural next question to ask is: *which attacking routines are most effective against a certain defensive set-up?* We have refrained from providing an empirical answer to that question in this paper because of the limited size and scope of our data set. In a follow-up paper we will make use of a significantly larger sample of tracking data to empirically investigate the most effective strategies for boosting the quality and quantity of chances created in corner kick situations.

Acknowledgments. We acknowledge Devin Pleuler at Toronto FC for his advice and insights, and Tiago Maia and Jan Schimpchen from SL Benfica for helping to produce the training data for our defensive role classification model.

References

1. Power, P., Hobbs, J., Ruiz, H., Wei, X., Lucey, P.: Mythbusting set-pieces in soccer. In: MIT Sloan Sports Analytics Conference (2018)
2. Beare, H., Stone, J.A.: Analysis of attacking corner kick strategies in the fa women's super league 2017/2018. Int. J. Perform. Anal. Sport **19**(6), 893–903 (2019)
3. Casal, C.A., Maneiro, R., Ardá, T., Losada, J.L., Rial, A.: Analysis of corner kick success in elite football. Int. J. Perform. Anal. Sport **15**(2), 430–451 (2015)
4. Pulling, C.: Long corner kicks in the English premier league: deliveries into the goal area and critical area. Kinesiol. Int. J. Fundam. Appl. Kinesiol. **47**(2), 193–201 (2015)
5. Pulling, C., Newton, J.: Defending corner kicks in the English premier league: near-post guard systems. Int. J. Perform. Anal. Sport **17**(3), 283–292 (2017)
6. Dempster, A.P., Laird, N.M., Rubin, D.B.: Maximum likelihood from incomplete data via the EM algorithm. J. Roy. Stat. Soc.: Ser. B (Methodol.) **39**(1), 1–22 (1977)
7. Hastie, T., Tibshirani, R., Friedman, J.: The Elements of Statistical Learning. SSS. Springer, New York (2009). https://doi.org/10.1007/978-0-387-84858-7
8. Kuang, D., Choo, J., Park, H.: Nonnegative matrix factorization for interactive topic modeling and document clustering. In: Celebi, M.E. (ed.) Partitional Clustering Algorithms, pp. 215–243. Springer, Cham (2015). https://doi.org/10.1007/978-3-319-09259-1_7
9. Lee, D.D., Seung, H.S.: Algorithms for non-negative matrix factorization. In: Advances in Neural Information Processing Systems, pp. 556–562 (2001)
10. Chen, T., Guestrin, C.: Xgboost: a scalable tree boosting system. In: Proceedings of the 22nd ACM SIGKDD International Conference on Knowledge Discovery and Data Mining, pp. 785–794 (2016)
11. Sagi, O., Rokach, L.: Ensemble learning: a survey. Wiley Interdisc. Rev. Data Mining Knowl. Discov. **8**(4), e1249 (2018)
12. Carling, C., Williams, A.M., Reilly, T.: Handbook of Soccer Matchanalysis: A Systematic Approach to Improving Performance. Psychology Press, London (2005)
13. Sarmento, H., Marcelino, R., Anguera, M.T., CampaniÇo, J., Matos, N., LeitÃo, J.C.: Match analysis in football: a systematic review. J. Sports Sci. **32**(20), 1831–1843 (2014)

How Data Availability Affects the Ability to Learn Good xG Models

Pieter Robberechts$^{(\boxtimes)}$ and Jesse Davis

Department of Computer Science, KU Leuven, Leuven, Belgium
{pieter.robberechts,jesse.davis}@cs.kuleuven.be

Abstract. Motivated by the fact that some shots are better than others, the expected goals (xG) metric attempts to quantify the quality of goal-scoring opportunities in soccer. The metric is becoming increasingly popular, making its way to TV analysts' desks. Yet, a vastly underexplored topic in the context of xG is how these models are affected by the data on which they are trained. In this paper, we explore several data-related questions that may affect the performance of an xG model. We showed that the amount of data needed to train an accurate xG model depends on the complexity of the learner and the number of features, with up to 5 seasons of data needed to train a complex gradient boosted trees model. Despite the style of play changing over time and varying between leagues, we did not find that using only recent data or league-specific models improves the accuracy significantly. Hence, if limited data is available, training models on less recent data or different leagues is a viable solution. Mixing data from multiple data sources should be avoided.

1 Introduction

The number of shot attempts is one of the most basic and frequently used statistics in soccer to summarize the performance of a team, where the team which accumulated the most attempts is often seen as the one that dominated the game offensively. However, the aggregate number of shots can be a misleading metric, since it does not consider the quality of the goal-scoring opportunities from which these shots arise. For example, a penalty is certainly more likely to result in a goal than a long range shot.

To overcome the pitfalls from simply using the number of shots (or even the number of shots on target), soccer analysts have introduced the notion of expected goals (xG) [8], where the main idea is to assign a quality metric on each shot. To do so, an expected-goals model assigns a value between zero and one to each shot which represents the probability that the shot will result in a goal. This is done by applying a machine learning classifier to a large historical data set of goal scoring opportunities. The classifier learns to distinguish big chances that are most likely to result in a goal from desperate shot attempts, based on features such as the shot's location, the body part used to kick the ball and the game situation (open-play, following a cross, free kick, etc.).

U. Brefeld et al. (Eds.): MLSA 2020, CCIS 1324, pp. 17–27, 2020.
https://doi.org/10.1007/978-3-030-64912-8_2

Allowing for a deeper and more insightful analysis of soccer players' shot attempts, xG has grown to be one of the most commonly used and best understood advanced metrics in soccer analytics. Yet, all existing research has focused on identifying the features that are indicative of a shot's quality [2,9,10] or interpreting the results obtained from this statistic [6,7].

A vastly underexplored topic in the context of xG is how these models are affected by the data on which they are trained. Training data varies from a single season [6] up to six seasons of data from multiple leagues [11]. Knowing that shot locations and efficiency vary between leagues and have evolved over time [13], the question is how the choice of training data affects the xG metric. Hence, in this paper, we will look at using event stream data to answer the following four questions:

1. How much data is needed to train an accurate xG model?
2. Does data go out of date? That is, does training a model using data from more recent seasons result in improved performance compared to using data from older seasons?
3. What is the effect of training an xG model using data from multiple leagues on performance? Does training a league-specific xG model result in improved performance?
4. What is the effect of training an xG model using data from multiple data sources on performance?

2   Data

Our data set consists of match event stream data from all matches between the 2012/2013 and 2018/2019 seasons in the English Premier League, the German Bundesliga, the Spanish LaLiga, the Italian Serie A, the French Ligue 1 and the Dutch Eredivisie. This event stream data was encoded in the SPADL format [4], which was specifically designed to enable automatic data analysis. From these event streams, we extracted all shots from open play (hence omitting penalties and direct free kicks[1]) and the two actions before each shot to capture the shot's context.

3   Methodology

Our goal is not to explore the complete space of design choices to arrive at the best possible xG model, but to mimic reasonable setups. To this end, we will consider two feature sets and two standard models.

---

[1] Since penalties and free-kicks are relatively easy to predict, our xG models might seem less accurate than other models which include these penalty and free-kick shots.

3.1 Features

Learning an accurate xG model requires coming up with a good set of features to describe the shot attempt. In this study, we consider two features sets: a basic feature set which encodes only the location of the shot and whether it was a header or regular shot, and an advanced feature set which adds contextual information about the preceding actions.

1. Basic Features. This simply consists of the following 5 features about the shot attempt: the x and y location of the shot, the distance to the center of the goal, the angle to the goal, and the body part used to take the shot (i.e., head or foot). The angle to the goal is measured as the width of goal mouth available to the shooter:

$$\theta = \arctan\left(\frac{\text{goal\_width} * x}{x^2 + y^2 - (\text{goal\_width}/2)^2}\right), \tag{1}$$

where x and y are the coordinates of the shot.

2. Advanced Features. This consists of 47 features constructed using the shot itself plus the previous two actions. These features encode the velocity of the possession, whether the assist was a through ball or a corner, whether the ball changed possession, etc. Specifically, we compute the following features for each shot and the two preceding actions. Features labelled with an asterisk are not computed for the shot itself, since they would leak information about its outcome.

Action type* The type of the action (pass, cross, shot, dribble, ...)
Body part The body part used to perform the action (foot or head)
Result* The result of the action (success or fail)
Start location The x, y location where the action starts
End location* The x, y location where the action ends
Start polar The polar coordinates of the location where the action starts
End polar* The polar coordinates of the location where the action ends
Team Whether the same team had possession during the previous action(s)
Space delta Displacement during the previous action(s)
Time delta Elapsed time since the previous action(s)
Speed Displacement during the previous action(s), normalized for elapsed time
Goal angle The angle to the goal, as defined in Eq. 1.

3.2 Evaluation Metrics

We believe that the primary objective of an expected goals model should be to produce calibrated probability estimates [5]. That is, the predicted probabilities should correspond to what is expected to happen in reality: when a shot is given an xG value of 0.3, this essentially means that if that one shot was taken a hundred times, it is expected to result in a goal 30 times. However, this cannot be assessed for a single shot, since each shot is taken only once. Therefore, one typically groups shots with similar xG values in bins and calculates the fraction of shots in each bin that actually resulted in a goal. Ideally, in the bin containing xG values of about x%, about x% of the shots should have resulted in a goal. This is reflected in the probability calibration curve in Fig. 1.

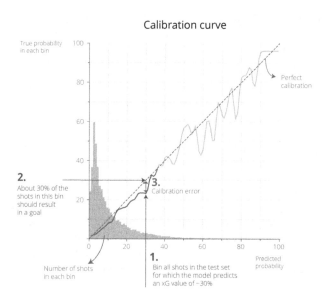

Fig. 1. Probability calibration curve of an xG model.

Many past works do not evaluate the calibration of their models and report the area under the ROC curve (AUROC). However, AUROC only considers the relative ranking of examples (i.e., whether one shot is more or less likely to result in a goal than another shot) and ignores the actual predicted probabilities. This means that a classifier can be poorly calibrated, yet still achieve an excellent AUROC. In contrast, we will report the Brier score [1][2]:

$$\text{Brier} = \frac{1}{\#\text{shots}} \sum_{i=1}^{\#\text{shots}} (\text{xG}_i - O_i)^2 \qquad (2)$$

where xG_i is the predicted xG value of shot i and O_i is 1 if shot results in a goal and 0 otherwise. This is a proper scoring rule that can only be minimized by reporting well-calibrated probabilities. While we would like to stress that we do not find AUROC to be an appropriate choice for evaluating xG models, we

---

[2] This version of the Brier score is only valid for binary classification. The original definition by Brier is applicable to multi-category classification as well.

will report it as many past works have used AUROC to evaluate xG models so it may help place what we have done in context.

3.3   Model Learning

We trained two machine learning models: a logistic regression model [12] and a gradient boosted tree model [3]. From a technical perspective, any model that returns a probability would be suitable, but these two models are most commonly used in practice. The key difference between a logistic regression model and a gradient boosted tree model is that the latter model can represent more fine-grained differences between goal scoring opportunities.

The hyperparameters of both models were tuned on the 2012/2013 and 2013/2014 seasons of the top-5 European leagues, using a grid search with 5-fold cross-validation. This hyperparameter tuning was done separately for both feature sets. The parameters which resulted in the best Brier score are listed in Appendix 8. The source code and trained models are available at https://github.com/ML-KULeuven/soccer_xg.

4   How Much Data is Needed to Train an Accurate xG model?

Figure 2 plots the Brier score for all shots in the 2018/2019 Premier League season as a function of the number of shot attempts included in the training set. This training set is constructed by randomly sampling shots from the 2012/2013 to 2017/2018 Premier League seasons. Because the training set differs for each sample size, we repeat this process 10 times and report the mean ± std Brier score for each sample size.

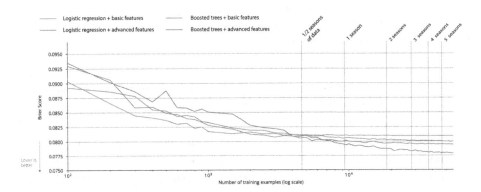

Fig. 2. Mean Brier scores on the 2018/2019 season of the English Premier League using random samples of increasing amounts of training data from the 2012/2013 to 2017/2018 seasons of the same league. The more complex models with the more expressive feature sets require more data, but eventually reach a better Brier score too.

The performance of a logistic regression model using the basic feature set converges after around 6,000 shots which is about 2/3 of a season of data. In contrast, the more complicated feature set requires about three times more data to converge. Of course, the more expressive feature set also results in better performance. Similarly, the more expressive gradient boosting model is more accurate and needs more data than the logistic regression model to converge. On the advanced feature set, it still slightly improves after five seasons of data.

From a machine learning perspective, these findings correspond to common knowledge. Typically, you want more examples than features so when you restrict the size of the feature set you need less data to train an accurate model. Similarly, training more complex models like gradient boosted ensembles requires more data than simpler models like logistic regression.

5   Does Data Go Out of Date?

Conventional wisdom is that more recent data is more valuable than older data. Moreover, data may eventually go out of date. In soccer, the style of play changes over time. Thus, it is possible that the types and quality of shot attempts may vary over time. For example in the Premier League, both the number of shots and the average distance of shots has decreased in the past six seasons [13]. Moreover, a player's skill or ability to convert the attempts may also change.

In this vein, we now evaluate the effect of using older data to train an xG model on its performance. In this experiment, the shots from the 2018/2019 Premier League season serve as the test set. We use two consecutive seasons of Premier League data to form the training set and vary the years used, progressively making them older. The below table shows the Brier scores for all four of the models on this experiment (Table 1):

Table 1. Brier scores on the 2018/2019 season of the English Premier League using pairs of increasingly older seasons of the same league as training data. Using old data results in only a negligible performance hit.

Training seasons	Basic features		Advanced features	
	Logistic regression	XGBoost	Logistic regression	XGBoost
2016/17, 2017/18	0.0812	0.0806	0.0783	0.0783
2015/16, 2016/17	0.0812	0.0804	0.0786	0.0786
2014/15, 2015/16	0.0813	0.0803	0.0790	0.0790
2013/14, 2014/15	0.0813	0.0803	0.0789	0.0789
2012/13, 2013/14	0.0813	0.0803	0.0802	0.0802

Interestingly, using old data results in only a negligible performance hit. Perhaps we would need a much longer historical window to see larger changes in performance.

6   Are xG Models League-Specific?

Different leagues have different styles of play. However, given that more data enables learning more accurate models, there is a tendency to combine data across different leagues when training a model. The question is what effect does this have? Would training a league-specific model result in better performance?

To answer this question, we consider data from the top-5 European leagues and the Dutch league. We create one test set for each league that consists of data from the 2018/2019 season and vary the data in the training set, considering three types of models:

1. A league-specific model that uses only data from the same league as the test set
2. A mixed model that uses data from the league in the test set plus other leagues, which is the standard approach
3. A model that uses only data from other leagues

To ensure that these training sets are of equivalent size, we always take a random sample of 14,460 shot attempts from 2 seasons of data, which is the largest common subset among these leagues.

In contrast to what others have found [2], the league on which the models are trained does not seem to have a big influence on the models' accuracy (Fig. 3). The league-specific model, mixed model and model trained on data from the other leagues perform equally on all leagues. Although these leagues definitely have different styles of play, these seem not to affect the scoring probabilities of a shot. This might be different in lower-level leagues where players have less intrinsic qualities, or in women's soccer.

Which league is in the test set is much more significant: shots in the Dutch league seem much harder to predict than shots in the Serie A. In terms of AUROC scores, the Dutch league is even a clear outlier. Perhaps scoring is more affected by luck in the Dutch league, being a lower-level league and having less skilled players.

7   Are Results Affected by the Data Source?

It is worth noting that each data source has its own data quality problems and uses different definitions for labeling shots. These data quality issues are related to the tracking of the events by human annotators who have to determine the right location and type of each event. This is hard to do, especially in a near real-time setting. Therefore, the locations of shots can vary up to a couple of meters between data providers.

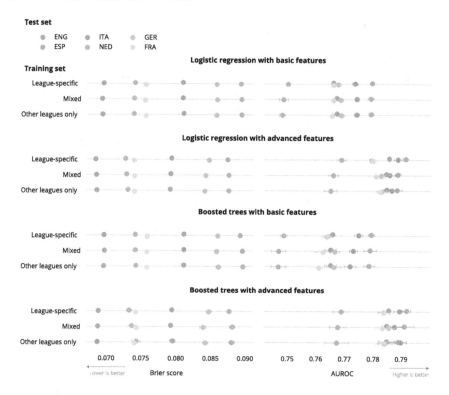

Fig. 3. Mean ± std Brier and AUROC scores on the 2018/2019 season of the English, Spanish, Italian, Dutch, German and French top leagues using 10 equal size random samples of training data from the same league (league-specific), all leagues (mixed) and other leagues only. The league on which the models are trained does not have a significant effect on the models' accuracy.

These differences may affect the classifiers and the conclusions derived from their outputs. Therefore, we repeated the earlier experiments with a second data provider. Although the data accuracy and event definitions can have a small impact on the reported Brier and AUROC score, the general conclusions in terms of data needed, recency and league effects remain valid. However, mixing data from different sources is not a good idea. This is illustrated in Fig. 4, where we repeat the experiment from Sect. 6 varying the data source in the training set instead of the league. Training xG models on data from the other provider, or mixing data from multiple providers results in a decreased performance.

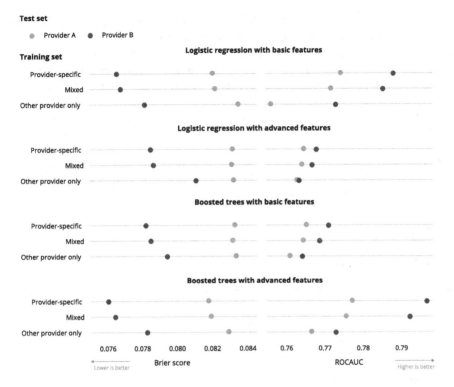

Fig. 4. Mean ± std Brier and AUROC scores on the 2018/2019 season of the English, Spanish, Italian, Dutch, German and French top leagues using 10 equal size random samples of training data from the same data provider (league-specific), both providers (mixed) and the other provider only. Training on data from a different source or mixing data from multiple sources results in decreased performance.

8   Discussion and Conclusions

In this study we have explored several data-related questions that may affect the performance of an xG model. These issues tend not to be extensively discussed in soccer analytics literature (at least publicly). We showed that the amount of data needed to train an accurate xG model depends on the complexity of the learner and the number of features, with up to 5 seasons of data needed to train a complex gradient boosted trees model. Despite the style of play changing over time and varying between leagues, we did not find that using only recent data or league-specific models improves the accuracy significantly. Hence, if limited data is available, training models on less recent data or different leagues is a viable solution.

In terms of evaluation, we advocated the use of Brier scores instead of AUROC. The applications of xG rely on the predicted probabilities, while the AUROC only measures whether the classifier is able to discriminate between failed and successful shot attempts. The Brier score, on the other hand, is a proper scoring rule that is affected by both discrimination and calibration. The importance of choosing the right metric is further illustrated by the fact that some models perform better on AUROC but worse on the Brier score and the other way around (Fig. 3). First, they both measure different qualities of the model and the Brier score is simply better at capturing the qualities that we need. Second, the AUROC can be sensitive to class imbalance [14]. Hence, the AUROC scores may be affected by the fraction of shot attempts that results in a goal in each league.

Acknowledgements. This research received funding from the KU Leuven Research Fund (C14/17/070) and the Flemish Government under the "Onderzoeksprogramma Artificiële Intelligentie (AI) Vlaanderen" programme.

A Hyperparameters

Logistic Regression + Basic Features

```
LogisticRegression(C=1.4174741629268048, class_weight=None, dual=False,
                   fit_intercept=True, intercept_scaling=1, l1_ratio=None,
                   max_iter=10000, multi_class='auto', n_jobs=None,
                   penalty='l2', random_state=None, solver='lbfgs', tol=0.0001,
                   verbose=0, warm_start=False)
```

XGBoost + Basic Features

```
XGBClassifier(base_score=0.6617525794305433, booster=None,
              colsample_bylevel=0.7545715311191046, colsample_bynode=1,
              colsample_bytree=0.8620890848654332, gamma=0.8215141264974605,
              gpu_id=-1, importance_type='gain', interaction_constraints=None,
              learning_rate=0.08, max_delta_step=0, max_depth=3,
              min_child_weight=8, missing=nan, monotone_constraints=None,
              n_estimators=100, n_jobs=0, num_parallel_tree=1,
              objective='binary:logistic', random_state=0,
              reg_alpha=0.4953861571782162, reg_lambda=9.636709165264326,
              scale_pos_weight=1.015057505195135, subsample=0.7667216094789041,
              tree_method=None, validate_parameters=False, verbosity=None)
```

Logistic Regression + Advanced Features

```
LogisticRegression(C=0.04328761281083057, class_weight=None, dual=False,
                   fit_intercept=True, intercept_scaling=1, l1_ratio=None,
                   max_iter=10000, multi_class='auto', n_jobs=None,
                   penalty='l2', random_state=None, solver='lbfgs', tol=0.0001,
                   verbose=0, warm_start=False)
```

XGBoost + Advanced Features

```
XGBClassifier(base_score=0.7590179091419386, booster=None,
              colsample_bylevel=0.8558659606677331, colsample_bynode=1,
              colsample_bytree=0.9437207946618666, gamma=0.2986963828079735,
```

```
gpu_id=-1, importance_type='gain', interaction_constraints=None,
learning_rate=0.08, max_delta_step=0, max_depth=4,
min_child_weight=6, missing=nan, monotone_constraints=None,
n_estimators=100, n_jobs=0, num_parallel_tree=1,
objective='binary:logistic', random_state=0,
reg_alpha=0.7495409923361984, reg_lambda=7.956623710511393,
scale_pos_weight=1.0211256886100497, subsample=0.7790327445095349,
tree_method=None, validate_parameters=False, verbosity=None)
```

References

1. Brier, G.W.: Verification of forecasts expressed in terms of probability. Mon. Weather Rev. **78**(1), 1–3 (1950)
2. Caley, M.: Premier league projections and new expected goals (2015). Accessed 27 May 2020. https://cartilagefreecaptain.sbnation.com/2015/10/19/9295905/premier-league-projections-and-new-expected-goals
3. Chen, T., Guestrin, C.: XGBoost: a scalable tree boosting system. In: Proceedings of the 22nd ACM SIGKDD International Conference on Knowledge Discovery and Data Mining, KDD 2016, ACM, New York, NY, USA ,pp. 785–794 (2016). https://doi.org/10.1145/2939672.2939785
4. Decroos, T., Bransen, L., Van Haaren, J., Davis, J.: Actions speak louder than goals: Valuing player actions in soccer. In: Proceedings of the 25th ACM SIGKDD International Conference on Knowledge Discovery & Data Mining, pp. 1851–1861 (2019)
5. Decroos, T., Davis, J.: Interpretable prediction of goals in soccer. In: Proceedings of the AAAI-20 Workshop on Artificial Intelligence in Team Sports, December 2019
6. Fairchild, A., Pelechrinis, K., Kokkodis, M.: Spatial analysis of shots in MLS: a model for expected goals and fractal dimensionality. J. Sports Anal. **4**(3), 165–174 (2018)
7. Gelade, G.: Which team formations produce the most expected goals? July 2017. http://business-analytic.co.uk/blog/which-team-formations-produce-the-most-expected-goals/
8. Green, S.: Assessing the performance of premier league goalscorers, April 2012. https://www.optasportspro.com/news-analysis/assessing-the-performance-of-premier-league-goalscorers/
9. Ijtsma, S.: A close look at my new expected goals model, August 2015. http://www.11tegen11.com/2015/08/14/a-close-look-at-my-new-expected-goals-model/
10. Kullowatz, M.: Expected goals 3.0 methodology, April 2015. https://www.americansocceranalysis.com/home/2015/4/14/expected-goals-methodology
11. Manfredi, G.: Expected goals & player analysis, May 2019. https://www.kaggle.com/gabrielmanfredi/expected-goals-player-analysis
12. Pedregosa, F., et al.: Scikit-learn: machine learning in Python. J. Mach. Learn. Res. **12**, 2825–2830 (2011)
13. Statsbomb: Danish football analysis, April 2019. https://divisionsforeningen.dk/wp-content/uploads/2019/04/Superliga_Analysis.pdf
14. Webb, G.I., Ting, K.M.: On the application of ROC analysis to predict classification performance under varying class distributions. Mach. Learn. **58**(1), 25–32 (2005)

Low-Cost Optical
Tracking of Soccer Players

Gabor Csanalosi[1], Gergely Dobreff[1], Alija Pasic[1], Marton Molnar[1],
and László Toka[1,2(✉)]

[1] Budapest University of Technology and Economics, Budapest, Hungary
{csanalosi,dobreff,pasic,molnar}@tmit.bme.hu
[2] MTA-BME Information Systems Research Group, Budapest, Hungary
toka@tmit.bme.hu

Abstract. Sports analytics are on the rise in European football, however, due to the high cost so far only the top tier leagues and champi-
onships have had the privilege of collecting high precision data to build
upon. We believe that this opportunity should be available for every-
one especially for youth teams, to develop and recognize talent earlier.
We therefore set the goal of creating a low-cost player tracking system
that could be applied in a wide base of football clubs and pitches, which
in turn would widen the reach for sports analytics, ultimately assisting
the work of scouts and coaches in general. In this paper, we present a
low-cost optical tracking solution based on cheap action cameras and
cloud-deployed data processing. As we build on existing research results
in terms of methods for player detection, i.e., background-foreground separation, and for tracking, i.e., Kalman filter, we adapt those algorithms
with the aim of sacrificing as least as possible on accuracy while keeping
costs low. The results are promising: our system yields significantly better accuracy than a standard deep learning based tracking model at the
fraction of its cost. In fact, at a cost of \$2.4 per match spent on cloud
processing of videos for real-time results, all players can be tracked with
a 11-meter precision on average.

Keywords: Sports analytics · Computer vision · Player tracking ·
Football

1 Introduction

Data analytics in sports has been gaining steam: with novel means of collecting
data, applying creative data mining methods and the rise of cloud-deployed big
data technologies, both the complexity and the importance of sports analytics,
especially in team sports, are steeply increasing. The predominant fraction of
sports analytics findings, more complex than box score and play-by-play statistics, rely on the positional data of players throughout the game, whether the
investigation targets a team or an individual sport.

In order to produce the position of sports players with fine time granularity and high accuracy, various high-precision player tracking solutions are used.

© Springer Nature Switzerland AG 2020
U. Brefeld et al. (Eds.): MLSA 2020, CCIS 1324, pp. 28–39, 2020.
https://doi.org/10.1007/978-3-030-64912-8_3

The two main categories of those solutions are: systems that apply wearable devices on the players, and optical tracking solutions that are based on multiple cameras' feeds and video processing techniques. Nowadays both categories consist of relatively expensive machinery and expertise, which restricts the usage of those solutions solely in the top level competitions.

In terms of costs, we argue that camera-based tracking can be made cheaper by sacrificing the video quality, but leveraging on today's low prices of cloud computing for processing the video. Instead of installing high quality custom camera arrays [2] and spidercams [18], one can install regular action cameras. Moreover, only a few of them might be enough, positioned as to get a bird's-eye view over more or less the whole play area, in case of football, the whole pitch. If the necessary elevation of the cameras allows to install them among the seats of a modest stadium, then the negligible installation costs, compared to what any currently available optical tracking product would cost, would make sports analytics widespread down to regional leagues quite rapidly. Of course on the one hand, the price of compromising on the video quality dictates sophisticated object detection and tracking algorithms, on the other hand the economical operation requires cheap compute resources, i.e., cloud service.

In this paper we describe our proposed football player tracking system that grasps the vision of cheap sports analytics for the masses of all leagues. Our system builds upon cheap action cameras, a camera positioning that is feasible next to most football pitches, and video processing methods that can be economically deployed in the cloud. Our contribution is two-fold: i) in the object detection phase we apply such novel ideas as synchronizing camera feeds based on the match start whistle and profiling players by the color of their jerseys; ii) we made custom modifications and parameter optimization of Kalman filter and data association based methods for tracking the players, and compared their performance with deep learning based solutions.

2 Player Detection

In this section we present the steps we made in order to determine the positions of players with high time granularity and accuracy based on the relatively poor video input we got from the low angle positioned cameras. We used two affordable sport cameras, and we placed them along the sideline (depicted in Fig. 1).

2.1 Time Synchronization of Camera Feeds

In a multi-camera system the first task is the synchronization of the videos. We recorded the videos with sound, thus we were able to use the starting whistle blow of the referee to synchronize the two camera feeds, i.e., the whistle sound is used as a movie clapper. We took advantage of its unique spectral component: we wrote a `python` script to perform a Fourier transformation [13] on the signal, and to seek peaks in the frequency spectrum. When the program attains the starting whistle sound, it removes the record before that sound for each file, and its result will be two video sequences with the same starting point.

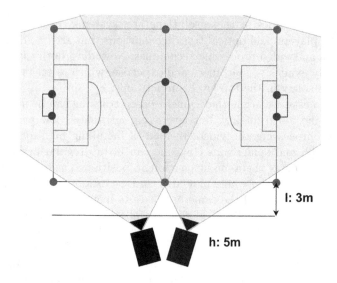

Fig. 1. Camera setup (Color figure online)

2.2   Playfield Detection

Playfield detection is one of most important preprocessing steps in detection
and tracking process. Several studies have appeared in this domain. In order to
tackle the drawbacks of RGB based field recognition [12,15] and edge detection
based methods [11], we have appointed the corner points on the two sides of
the field. In the first step, we took a frame from the videos and undistorted
them with the distortion matrix of the camera lens to get straight lines on the
image. In the second step, we calculated the corner pixels for each side: we
located the intersection of the center line and the center circle and the bottom
of the goal posts (red dots on Fig. 1). From these four points, we calculated
the necessary four corner points (green dots on Fig. 1) with the use of the
Cross-ratio method [8]. Based on this idea, with these estimated corner pixels
the future transformations will generate more accurate two-dimensional position
coordinates than the ones we could get from the image. This method is semi-
automatic: the calculation is automatic, but the basepoint selection is manual.

2.3   Masking

Player detection is a broad research area in sport video analysis. It can be
based on Histogram of Oriented Gradients (HOG) [11], or some feature selection
algorithms such as dominant color-based background subtraction [9], and edge
detection [3]. Since our videos were recorded from stationary points, we opted
for a movement-based background-foreground separation [6] method to separate
moving objects from the background. This method is based on the Gaussian
mixture model: it sets up multiple Gaussian distribution models for each pixel,

then the algorithm estimates a corresponding confidence value for each Gaussian distribution model, and selects the best model according to the descending confidence order. With the selected distribution model, the algorithm is able to assess whether the pixel is a foreground or a background one.

After the optimization of the "length of the history", i.e., the frame number that gives the length of the model's input dataset, the method separates the players from the field without their shadows, and the mask contains only a small amount of noise. As it is noticeable in Fig. 2, the noisy regions are distributed on the field, that is why there is no massive noise junction in the size of a player. This method is faster than any AI method that we have tested in our servers, and is capable of real-time video processing with sufficient number of CPU cores.

Fig. 2. Separated mask

2.4 Dynamic Validation

As mentioned in Sect. 2.2, we used the Cross-ratio method [8] to calculate corner coordinates. The method is based on a theory that if four points lie on a straight line (and are projected to an image) and we know their distances, i.e., the actual distance in meters and in pixels on the image, we can calculate an unknown distance on the projected line between any two points in pixels. This method can be used to make a grid on the field with cells, which have the same size in real life. After calculating the grid, we can select a random point in it, and obtain the cell, which contains the point. As the cell's size is known (in meters) and we can calculate the length of the cell sides on the image in pixels, we can determine the pixel range, which is the size of an average football player there.

With this pixel range, we can validate each object in the foreground mask, with the length of their bounding boxes. This method is efficient since we can calculate the grid beforehand. The method obtains for the enclosing cell the blob and links it to the grid cell. For each grid cell corner, we calculate the ideal size of a player on the image. Nonetheless, the calculated player size may vary around the ideal value within a predefined range, therefore the validation could confirm bounding boxes, which contain more than one player. i.e., occlusion. Our method validates more than 95% of the players on the mask, and it generates less than 1% false-positive detection. We created a histogram to illustrate the distribution of the number of recognized players on a video frame, shown in Fig. 3 (left plot).

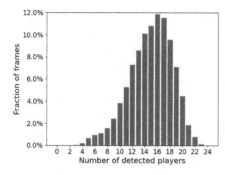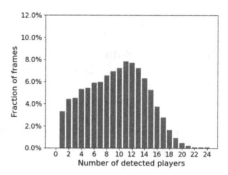

Fig. 3. Histogram of the number of detected players per frame yielded by our proposed method (left), and by a deep learning framework (right)

2.5   Perspective Transformation

After player detection, we have the positions of the players in the image. However, this position is given in pixels and it is in a projected coordinate system. Of course, our goal is to get the real-life coordinates of the players, which can be utilized for analytic purposes. We therefore perform a perspective transformation [14]. In [4] the real transformation of 3D to 2D camera calibration with projection matrix is obtained by plane-to-plane homography, i.e., a standard computer vision procedure for combining two images of the same planar surface in space, and the transformation of the players from image coordinates to real world coordinates is performed by using the inverse of homography H^{-1}, where H is the homography matrix. We improve the transformation by proposing a novel algorithm to get the top-down, bird's eye view of an image. In the first step, we calculate the transformation matrix, which represents the connection between the corresponding corner points on the image, and on the virtual two-dimensional field. The corner points of the half courts on the image were calculated before the background-foreground separation, and they are calculated for both sides. To determine the size of the virtual field, we have to estimate or find the size of the actual football pitch since the UEFA certified fields vary in sizes. In order to avoid the rounding loss, we calculate the size of the virtual field with the smallest common division of the pitch size in pixels and the actual field size in meters. From these values, we can create the transformation matrix, and with matrix multiplication, the program will transform the player's positions on the virtual field to the real-life positions. From these real-life coordinates, with a simple multiplication, the program calculates the positions in meters.

2.6   Additional Color Information

So far we presented the process of player recognition and coordinate transformation, however, these methods are not sufficient to generate enough information for player identification. The self-evident way to identify a player is to separate them based on the color of their jersey. Each team has a unique jersey color which is easily separable from the other teams in a match. We implemented a function with inputs of the dominant colors of the two jerseys to create the masks with these given colors, and to measure the quantity of these colors on the masks. If one of these colors appears in a significant amount in the masked player, the player is assumed to belong to the given team.

With these six main steps our application generates positional, size, and color information about the players on the pitch. The speed of our software depends on the positions of the players; currently our multi-thread detection program needs 1.5 s on average to process a frame on a 6-core CPU (Intel Xeon E5-2620v3).

3   Statistical Tracking Method

In this section we present a statistical method we used to track multiple players individually. The method is based on Kalman filters, and the obtained results that we also show are promising.

3.1   Our Kalman Filter Based Tracking Method

Using a Kalman filter is a common approach for tracking: in [7] the algorithm was tested for many purposes including soccer analysis, however it can be also applied for tracking pedestrians [16]. In general, Kalman filter is used to remove statistical noise from a system, which is in our case caused by the player recognition algorithm. The method takes the coordinates from the current frame and combines it with the current state to produce the next state of the system. The current state is determined by the previous state and the previous input. The Kalman filter is "light on memory", because it only stores one state and uses the current input, sequentially.

The algorithm we used was proposed by [17] for tracking multiple bugs. However, we expanded their implementation for our task with some features. Our Kalman filter based algorithm creates predictions of the next coordinates based on the current position, and a Hungarian method matches those predicted points with the actual measured points, if possible. When a considerably good assignment can be made, we keep the connection, otherwise the point is left unassigned, and it is dropped. If a tracked player is not detected in a few frames, we keep the Kalman filter's prediction for its position. Hence our algorithm usually creates points in the traces that are not produced directly by the transformation algorithm in Sect. 2.5: these are predicted positions based on the preceding trajectories.

3.2   Segmenting the Video Input for Better Tracking Results

Running the Kalman filter based algorithm for a long time may lead to results diverging from the real tracks, and eventually to losing the players altogether: after a while, the predicted points may start oscillating between different players.

On the other hand, the algorithm requires some time to determine the arrangement of the individual players. Therefore we had to optimize the length of the video segment for which we run the Kalman filter based tracking, and connect the produced traces with an association approach, e.g., with Hungarian method, between the consecutive video segments.

Therefore we measured the performance of the algorithm on different time intervals. We were able to realize the disadvantages of running the algorithm for longer intervals: the predicted points started oscillating heavily on any runtime longer than 90 s. However tracking for only 20 s did not produce meaningful tracks. So we decided to run the algorithm on 50 s intervals, and to connect these discrete trajectories with the Hungarian method. This latter was performed by calculating the distance between the last points of the tracks from a segment and the first points of the tracks in the subsequent segment, and using these distances in the cost-matrix for matching the tracks.

3.3   Tracking Accuracy

We compared the results of the player recognition and the Kalman filter based tracking algorithm with the original GPS coordinates from the players wearable sensors (from their Catapult vests [1]). We tested the algorithm for 2 matches. We calculated the minimum distances between the two sets of points, i.e., between GPS coordinates and the tracked points. The results are shown as cumulative distribution in Fig. 4, compared with the results of a deep learning tracking method. The high level statistics are: average distance is 11.6 m, the median of distance values is 9.0 m.

We are aware of the fact that without the correct identification of the players the distance from GPS positions might be misleading, e.g., the distance is false in cases where wrong trajectories are being compared. Therefore we turned to another metric for evaluation: the amount of tracks per frame. The histogram of followed tracks can be seen in Fig. 5 (left plot). We measured that the average of this metric is 9.8 for the 10 outfield players of a team in the observed 2 matches. We note that the missing recognition of players on the opposite side of the pitch may lead to oscillating tracks and bad results. However, the Kalman filter strives to fill in this missing information and predict where players could have been on the frames we could not detect them.

For validation we created a ground truth for 3 players during 60 s manually. Overall, all of the 3 measured players had an average minimum distance below 2 m by comparing their GPS coordinates with the outcome of the tracking. However, the player in the close range of the camera produced a 0.6-meter improvement compared to the player on the further side in this distance metric. This finding proves that the relatively high overall average is due to outliers in the empirical distribution of the distances shown in Fig. 4, potentially caused by missing detections. Therefore we also measured how many times a player loses its unique id that it is assigned to. This validation was also made by visual inspection. Based on this validation, the method can track one player successfully for around 30 s without losing its identity; results are displayed in Fig. 6.

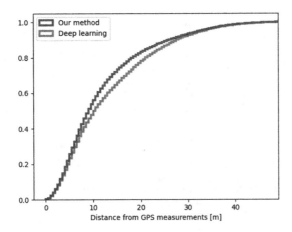

Fig. 4. Empirical cumulative distribution of minimum distances between tracked players and their GPS coordinates: the qualitative metric for our system and the baseline

3.4   Cost Evaluation

The cost of this tracking algorithm is fairly reasonable: the algorithm can process around 80–85 frames per second, using 1 CPU core (Intel Xeon E5-2620v3 CPU). Therefore running the algorithm for a match video input with a regular resolution, the tracking results can be obtained in real time with an affordable CPU.

In summary, with this method we are able to produce reliable individual tracks for players during the whole runtime, but the results are showing that tracking players far from the camera is challenging. Players covering separate regions in the pitch without having many teammates in that nearby area can be tracked efficiently, and nearly unambiguously. In most cases our method manages to track individuals without any errors within the segments and to fully connect the track segments successfully. For crowded situations however, it is inevitable that some errors are introduced. As a future task, we will tackle ID switches: we plan to determine the player identities backwards starting from the situations when players can be easily separated and recognized by their positions in the team. By doing this, we lose the online manner of processing the video input, but on the other hand, we can ensure that the followed tracks are matched to players correctly.

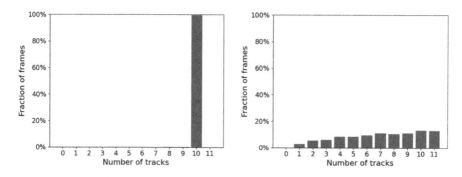

Fig. 5. Histogram of the number of tracks per frame yielded by our tracking method (left), and by a deep learning framework (right)

4 Deep Learning Based Tracking as Baseline

In order to compare our method with state-of-the-art solutions, for a baseline model we chose a deep learning method that best suited our use-case. Since we wanted to build a low-cost solution, we chose existing pre-trained models, as training such a neural network is a particularly costly procedure: both resources and labeled data are expensive.

4.1 Structure of the Baseline Model

Both parts of the task, player detection and player tracking, were performed using deep learning algorithms: we utilized the Detectron2 [20] for player detection, and then used the DeepSort [19] algorithm for tracking.

Detectron2 implements state-of-the-art object recognition algorithms, of which we use Faster R-CNN [5] (Region with Convolutional Neural Network). These algorithms are capable of detecting multiple object classes as they are trained on the COCO dataset [10]. This dataset contains the person class, so in fact the baseline model will look for a generic person object in the input images.

The DeepSort algorithm compares the detection results in the following frame with the tracked objects using two metrics. Deep appearance descriptors are created by using a pre-trained CNN on the cropped image of each detected object. This CNN was trained on a pedestrian re-identification dataset. In addition, the position of each track in the following frame is predicted by Kalman filter using the previous positions of the track. Then a distance metric is calculated based on the predicted position and the newly arrived detection. Using these two metrics the best detection is assigned for each track. In the original article [19], the authors concluded that omitting distance metrics to track pedestrians yields the best result. However, in our case, since the players on the same team look very similar, in Eq. 5 of [19] we set the λ parameter (which describes the ratio of the two metrics) to 0.6 based on our optimization results.

Hence, our baseline model consists of two parts: Faster R-CNN recognizes players on the incoming frame, and then passes the bounding box information

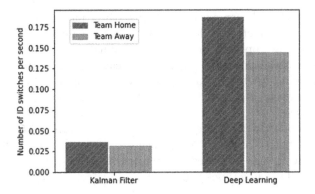

Fig. 6. The number of identity switches per second per player: the quantitative metric for our system and the baseline

to the DeepSort algorithm, which creates the above-mentioned metrics based on the boxes and associates the detection to the tracks, which are stored in memory.

4.2 Performance Evaluation and Cost

The baseline solution, i.e., the Faster R-CNN detection and DeepSort tracking, was examined on the same 2 matches as our proposed system. The false-negative detection of Faster R-CNN was very high because distant players and players in unusual poses - such as while jumping - were not recognized. The average number of detected players per frame for the test videos is 5 per team which is significantly poorer than our system's result, i.e., 7. The histogram of detected players by both methods are depicted in Fig. 3. The median distance between the players detected on the image and the GPS coordinates is 10.5 m (to be compared to 9.0 m of our solution). The empirical cumulative distribution of the distances for the two methods, i.e., our system and DeepSort, is shown in Fig. 4. Our solution's results seem to be slightly more precise in this evaluation aspect. The advantage becomes obvious when we take a look at the third performance metric, the number of tracks per frame. In Fig. 5 the difference is clearly apparent: while our tracking method continuously tracks all players, the deep learning follows only a fraction of those in many frames. The DeepSort tracking maintained 9.3 tracks on average per frame in the 2 match videos for the 2 teams, goalkeepers (and referees) included; on average a track ended after 42 s.

The deep learning solution performed poorly in terms of ID switches as well. Even if the R-CNN model finds players accurately, based on GPS measurements the tracking is not effective because the tracks are often swapped. Therefore despite the fact that a track lives for a long time, it is often associated with multiple players. The number of ID switches in the three 60-second-long segments compared to our proposed method are shown in Fig. 6. It can be seen that the number of ID switches are much higher than in our proposed method. In particular, the Home team shows higher ID switches in both methods because their players moved on the far side of the pitch in those particular video segments, resulting in poorer detection. Additionally, we also examined the performance of the deep learning approach on the three manually annotated players. Our observation is that the closer the player to the camera, the better the tracking. During the tracking the three players suffered 44, 34 and 27 ID switches, and an ID lasted on average only for 1.6, 2.1, 2.5 s, a much worse result than our proposed system's.

We run the models on the same 6-core processor (Intel Xeon E5-2620v3 CPU) as the detection with 32GB of RAM. Since we did not use GPU to serve our low cost goal, the models processed one image extremely slowly: one frame took 4.6 s on average. That is 3 times higher than our detection's demand.

5   Conclusion

We presented a novel low-cost optical tracking system for soccer players, which is based on custom recognition methods, and Kalman filter and Hungarian algorithm for tracking. The main merit of the system is the exceptionally low-cost that is achieved through cloud computing (10 CPU cores for real-time processing 1 Hz rate video frames at a cost of $2.4 for a 90-min match from e.g., Amazon AWS) and by utilizing common sport cameras (e.g., 2 pieces of SJCAM SJ7 Star camera, each at $200). Despite the low cost, the accuracy of player recognition is surprisingly high. We compared our novel tracking method with an AI-based approach, and we demonstrated that our optical tracking method significantly outperformed it in both accuracy and resource consumption. We believe that our approach will enable low-cost analytics for the less wealthy clubs, too. The young talented players will be identified earlier and scouting itself will take a next step. The backward identification of players is ongoing work, and as a future work we plan to release the cloud-native implementation of our system as open source.

Acknowledgement. This work was supported by the National Research, Development and Innovation Office of Hungary (NKFIH) in research project FK 128233, financed under the FK_18 funding scheme.

References

1. Catapult: Wearable technology (2020). https://www.catapultsports.com/
2. ChyronHego: The leading sports tracking solution (2020). https://chyronhego. com/products/sports-tracking/tracab-optical-tracking/
3. Direkoglu, C., Sah, M., O'Connor, N.E.: Player detection in field sports. Mach. Vis. Appl. **29**(2), 187–206 (2017). https://doi.org/10.1007/s00138-017-0893-8
4. Gerke, S., Linnemann, A., Müller, K.: Soccer player recognition using spatial constellation features and jersey number recognition. Comput. Vis. Image Underst. **159**, 105–115 (2017). Elsevier
5. Girshick, R.: Fast R-CNN. In: Proceedings of the IEEE International Conference on Computer Vision, pp. 1440–1448 (2015)

6. Harville, M., Gordon, G., Woodfill, J.: Foreground segmentation using adaptive mixture models in color and depth. In: Proceedings IEEE Workshop on Detection and Recognition of Events in Video, pp. 3–11 (2001)

7. Kulkarni, A., Rani, E.: Kalman filter based multi object tracking system. Int. J. Electron. Commun. Instrum. Eng. Res. Dev. **8**(2), 1–6 (2018)

8. Lei, G.: Recognition of planar objects in 3-D space from single perspective views using cross ratio. IEEE Trans. Robot. Autom. **6**(4), 432–437 (1990)

9. Li, G., Zhang, C.: Automatic detection technology of sports athletes based on image recognition technology. EURASIP J. Image Video Process. **2019**(1), 1–9 (2019). https://doi.org/10.1186/s13640-019-0415-x

10. Lin, T.-Y., et al.: Microsoft COCO: common objects in context. In: Fleet, D., Pajdla, T., Schiele, B., Tuytelaars, T. (eds.) ECCV 2014. LNCS, vol. 8693, pp. 740–755. Springer, Cham (2014). https://doi.org/10.1007/978-3-319-10602-1_48

11. Maćkowiak, S., Konieczny, J., Kurc, M., Maćkowiak, P.: Football player detection in video broadcast. In: Bolc, L., Tadeusiewicz, R., Chmielewski, L.J., Wojciechowski, K. (eds.) ICCVG 2010. LNCS, vol. 6375, pp. 118–125. Springer, Heidelberg (2010). https://doi.org/10.1007/978-3-642-15907-7_15

12. Naushad Ali, M., Abdullah-Al-Wadud, M., Lee, S.L.: An efficient algorithm for detection of soccer ball and players. In: Signal Processing Image Processing and Pattern Recognition (2012)

13. Nussbaumer, H.J.: Fast Fourier Transform and Convolution Algorithms. Springer, Heidelberg (1981). https://doi.org/10.1007/978-3-642-81897-4

14. OpenCV: OpenCV provided geometric image transformations (2020). https://docs.opencv.org/2.4/modules/imgproc/doc/geometric_transformations.html

15. Rao, U., Pati, U.C.: A novel algorithm for detection of soccer ball and player. In: International Conference on Communications and Signal Processing (2015)

16. Shantaiya, S., Verma, K., Mehta, K.: Multiple object tracking using Kalman filter and optical flow.Eur. J. Adv. Eng. Technol. **2**(2), 34–39 (2015)

17. Sharma, A.: Multi object tracking with Kalman-filter (2018). https://github.com/mabhisharma/Multi-Object-Tracking-with-Kalman-Filter

18. Spidercam: Spidercam FIELD (2020). https://www.spidercam.tv/

19. Wojke, N., Bewley, A., Paulus, D.: Simple online and realtime tracking with a deep association metric. In: 2017 IEEE International Conference on Image Processing (ICIP), pp. 3645–3649 (2017)

20. Wu, Y., Kirillov, A., Massa, F., Lo, W.Y., Girshick, R.: Detectron2 (2019). https://github.com/facebookresearch/detectron2

An Autoencoder Based Approach to Simulate Sports Games

Ashwin Vaswani, Rijul Ganguly$^{(\boxtimes)}$, Het Shah, Sharan Ranjit S, Shrey Pandit, and Samruddhi Bothara

Birla Institute of Technology and Science Pilani, K. K. Birla Goa Campus, Goa, India
f20170971@goa.bits-pilani.ac.in

Abstract. Sports data has become widely available in the recent past. With the improvement of machine learning techniques, there have been attempts to use sports data to analyze not only the outcome of individual games but also to improve insights and strategies. The outbreak of COVID-19 has interrupted sports leagues globally, giving rise to increasing questions and speculations about the outcome of this season's leagues. What if the season was not interrupted and concluded normally? Which teams would end up winning trophies? Which players would perform the best? Which team would end their season on a high and which teams would fail to keep up with the pressure? We aim to tackle this problem and develop a solution. In this paper, we propose **UCLData**, which is a dataset containing detailed information of UEFA Champions League games played over the past six years. We also propose a novel autoencoder based machine learning pipeline that can come up with a story on how the rest of the season will pan out.

Keywords: Sports analytics · Machine learning · Data mining · Auto-encoder

1 Introduction

Sports analytics has received extensive attention over the past few years. While a lot of work in sports analysis emphasizes on visual [1,2] and tactical analysis [3], there have been recent attempts to predict the outcome of individual games and entire seasons. However, most of these attempts only predict the outcome without providing insights or internal statistics to corroborate their results. Another issue is the lack of large clean datasets for this task. While most of the existing datasets provide data summarising matches, there is little focus on the little intricacies of matches that might be of interest. To tackle this, our proposed **UCLData** dataset consists of both match and individual statistics from Champions League matches played over the past six years. Further, we handle dataset size issues with the help of some intuitive priors or handcrafted features which make our model robust and realistic.

In this work, our proposed novel autoencoder based architecture not only predicts the outcome of a game but also predicts its internal statistics, to give a

---

A. Vaswani, R. Ganguly, H. Shah and S. Sharan Ranjit—Equal contribution.

U. Brefeld et al. (Eds.): MLSA 2020, CCIS 1324, pp. 40–50, 2020.
https://doi.org/10.1007/978-3-030-64912-8_4

more holistic picture of how a match is expected to pan out. Moreover, apart from match-wise statistics, we also present player-wise statistics to provide details about the contribution of each player and minor details about a match which are generally ignored. The code for our work is made publicly available.[1]

2   Related Work

Most of the previous approaches based on machine learning for predicting results of sports games aim to predict simply the outcome of matches, instead of running a simulation predicting all match-related statistics.

Kampakis *et al.* [4] used both player and team data for cricket matches to predict the performance of teams based on different features. A study by Rotshtein *et al.* [5] used several predictive models to predict outcomes in the English Premier League and the Premiership Rugby in England. There are various works based on Bayesian models [6,7], but these limit themselves to predicting the outcomes of individual football matches instead of running simulations. A work based on the Gaussian Process model by L. Maystre *et al.* [8] attempts to learn the strengths and traits of a team by player wise contributions. This is an inspiration for our present study.

Huang *et al.* [9] focus on using neural networks to predict the results of the 2006 Football World Cup and this is the most similar to what we have tried to achieve in this paper. They achieved an accuracy of 76.9% on the games' results, having special difficulty in predicting draws. Hucaljuk *et al.* [10] incorporated expert opinion into Champions League matches, but in this case, there was no increase in accuracy in their prediction of game scores. S. Mohammad Arabzad *et al.* [11] incorporated the use of neural networks for the Iranian premier league. Flitman *et al.* [12] developed a model that will readily predict the winner of Australian Football League games together with the probability of that win. This model was developed using a genetically modified neural network to calculate the likely winner, combined with a linear program optimisation to determine the probability of that win occurring in the context of the tipping competition scoring regime.

3   Dataset

The following section details our approach for creating a dataset from which we can derive meaningful predictions.

3.1   Data Collection

We scrape data from the official UEFA Champions League website to build our dataset. Data from the years 2014 to 2020 is used. Overall we collect the data for 157 knockout stage matches. We do not collect data for group stage matches

---

[1] https://github.com/ashwinvaswani/whatif.

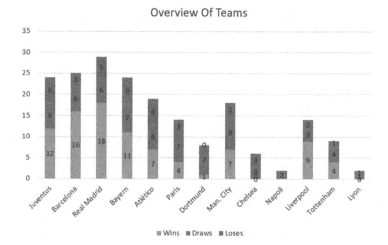

Fig. 1. Overview of Dataset

because our predictions will be on the knockout stage games of the 2019 − 20 season of the Champions League, and hence we did not want the context of group stage matches misleading our model.

To scrape the data, we use the Python library Beautiful Soup [13], which assists us to take the data directly from the relevant websites. We divide our data into two categories - team data and player data. Team data contains the statistics for the entire team playing in the match on both sides, while player data includes the statistics of the teams' individual players.

To obtain team data, we use the official UEFA website for the individual matches. However, the official website does not contain the statistics for individual players. Hence, we extract individual player data from the FBref website [14] and the Global Sports Archive website [15]. Table 1 summarises the attributes we considered for our dataset.

Table 1. List of attributes for a team and an player

	Attributes
Team	Total goals, total attempts, attempts on and off target, blocked shots, shots which hit the woodwork, corners, off-sides, amount of possession, total passes, passing accuracy, completed passes, distance covered, number of balls recovered, tackles, clearances, blocks, yellow and red cards, fouls.
Individual	Goals scored, total shots, shots on target, assists, interceptions, crosses, fouls committed, player off-sides, total time played

3.2   Data Pre-processing

Our data in its raw form contains numbers spanning a wide range - from hundreds in the fields such as passes completed to only one or two in areas such as goals. Passing such fields without any pre-processing would lead to our proposed model not accurately capturing this wide range. Hence we normalize our data to the range of zero to one using MinMax Scaling. This ensures that our model does not give any undue importance to any fields because of scaling issues. After pre-processing, we create embeddings from our normalized data.

3.3   Creation of Embeddings

There are some problems with using individual match data throughout. First, information from earlier matches cannot be used efficiently. This argument can be demonstrated with the help of an example. Let us say two teams A and B play against each other in years Y1 and Y2. Now, these two games are not independent as the two sides have played multiple other teams in this period and improved their game-play. Thus, it is not ideal to directly use individual match stats without capturing this context. Another issue is regarding players switching teams, which is quite common in sports. If a player plays in team A in year Y1 and switches to team B in year Y2, we need a way to represent it so that their individual information is maintained. We solve these problems with the use of embeddings. We create embeddings for each team and each player so that when two teams are matched up, these representations can capture the interactions with other teams and players and can preserve contextual information from previous data.

4   Methodology

4.1   Handling Problem of Data Bias

Our data consists of matches from the last six years of Champions League games. Although we found this data sufficient to capture relationships between teams and players, there were a few issues due to imbalance. Some teams, not being Champions League regulars, had fewer data points. We find that our initial results were biased towards the lower number of data points of these teams and lacked generalization. We attempted to overcome this issue with the help of prior information, which is important in the field of football analysis. We propose three additional hand-crafted features which are crucial in the context of a game. We also infer that regularisation and dropout help in solving some of these problems. We show in the following sections how the addition of each of these features helps in making our results more robust.

Home/Away Status: An important feature of Champions League knockout stages is the Home/Away concept. A fixture consists of two games wherein each game is played at the home ground of the two teams. The Fig. 2(a) shows some

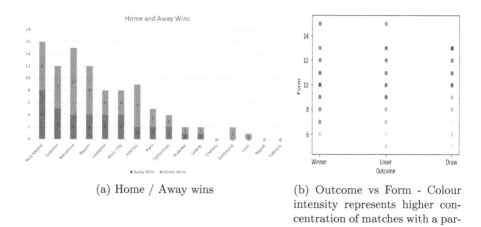

(a) Home / Away wins

(b) Outcome vs Form - Colour intensity represents higher concentration of matches with a particular outcome.

Fig. 2. Home/Away wins and Outcome vs Form

analysis of the importance of the location of the fixture. It can be seen that there is a general trend for most teams to perform better at home than while away, which is quite intuitive. We attempt to use this information by adding an extra flag to indicate the team is playing at home apart from our embeddings while giving input to the model.

Form Index: Another essential feature, relevant to the context of a match, is the form of the two teams playing. It can be seen in Fig. 2(b) that at lower values of the form(<7), teams are less likely to win whereas, in the middle range, it's difficult to predict with just form. We used the recent results of each team (Results from the five most recent games before the fixture) to generate a form index by giving a score of three points to a Win, one to a Draw, and zero to a Loss. This additional information helped in improving results of certain matches as a team would rather go into a game with a form of 15(five straight wins) than 0(five straight losses).

Experience: Figure 1 shows that some teams such as Real Madrid, being Champions League regulars have plenty of data points. In contrast, teams like Atalanta, who are new to the Champions League, have few data points. Hence, results of matches involving Atalanta were biased to the data from these limited games resulting in Atalanta performing exceptionally well against the odds in our initial experiments. While this can be considered a case of an "upset" or Atalanta being "dark horses", we wanted to improve our results and make our predictions robust. A critical factor is a team's experience in the Champions League, due to the pressure of playing in such a high-profile platform. We accumulated total matches played by every team in our data to account for this experience factor, which helped in solving the issue of predictions being biased because of limited data.

4.2   Details of the Model

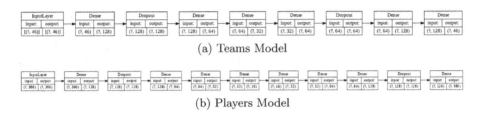

(a) Teams Model

(b) Players Model

Fig. 3. Details of the models used

Our network is based on the idea of autoencoders [16] which are widely used for data compression. The aim of our training process is to learn about the various features of the team and the players. To achieve this we aim to learn an embedding in latent dimension. We also want this data in latent dimension to be robust from other factors which cannot always be predicted from the data. The model architectures are as shown in Fig. 3. We add a Gaussian noise to this in order to create a "noisy" embedding. This is given as an input to the network. The intuition for adding Gaussian noise is that it will help take into consideration some factors which are not consistent with the data (example a player having a lucky day or an off day/weather conditions which affect the play). We use the embedding without Gaussian noise as our ground truth labels. The schematic of the training process is given in the Fig. 4. So, after the training process, the model learned some important insights about the team's/player's performance, which is later helpful during the playoffs to decide the winner of a particular match. For training, the loss is taken to be **mean squared error**, and the metric that we have considered is the **root mean squared error** (RMSE). We used Adam Optimizer with a learning rate of 0.01 and the batch size was 10 embeddings, for both our models. The RMSE values in the training and validation process are not metrics of performance of the model on new matches, rather they are indicators of the model's efficiency in learning the embedding. The training RMSE value for the team model is 0.1380, and for players model is 0.1127. The validation RMSE values for both the models are pretty close to the training models at 0.1379 for the team model and 0.1126 for the players' model. The overall summary of our pipeline can be seen in Fig. 4.

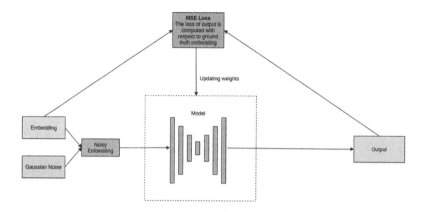

Fig. 4. Summary of our pipeline

5   Results and Observations

Fig. 5. Overview of simulation

Figure 5 gives an overview of the simulation of the interrupted knockout stages of Champions League 2019–20. Our model predicts both match(Total Goals, Total Passes, Possession, Blocks, Corners, etc.) and player statistics(Who scored the goals, Assists, Shots, Crosses, etc.) for the two teams in the fixture. The winner(team with a higher aggregate score over two legs) proceeds to the next round. In the case of a draw in the overall fixture (equal aggregate score from home/away legs), the team with the highest number of shots on target qualifies. We picked **Shots on target** as a decider, as it has the highest correlation with goals, which can be seen in Fig. 6(a).

The first simulation is between Bayern Munich and Chelsea(2nd Leg). Bayern Munich beat Chelsea comprehensively in the first leg fixture, which was

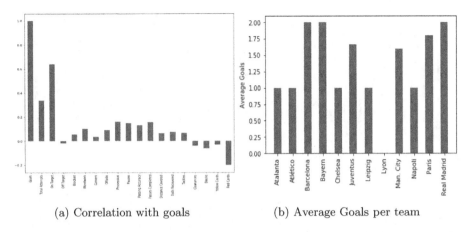

(a) Correlation with goals   (b) Average Goals per team

Fig. 6. (a) Shows high correlation between goals and shots on target (b) Identifies high/low scoring teams

conducted before the season was interrupted. Bayern entered the game with a form of five wins in its last five games, whereas Chelsea had mixed results recently. The odds favored Bayern to win this tie, which is also backed up by our results. Bayern beat Chelsea comfortably with a scoreline of 2–1 dominating the possession (57%) and total passing (597) stats. These stats are also backed up, as our data shows that Bayern Munich is one of the best teams in Europe in terms of passing and possession stats, which can be seen in Fig. 7(1a) and Fig. 7(2a). The goal scorers for Bayern were Robert Lewandowski and Jerome Boateng. Jorginho was the lone scorer for Chelsea. Our analysis shows Lewandowski as one of the most prolific goal scorers in Europe over the past few years, which is backed up by these results.

A similar result was found in the simulation of the game between Barcelona and Napoli. Barcelona being European giants and one of the best passers in Europe dominated the passing (571) and possession (56%) stats and won with a scoreline of 2–1 at home with Rakitic scoring for Barcelona. Rakitic has a good record of scoring in Champions League knockouts, which is an interesting observation that our model is able to capture. Also, Barcelona has a great home record, as can be seen in Fig. 1, which is also corroborated by our results.

In another match, Paris (PSG) beat Atlético by two goals to one in both fixtures. Our analysis shows that Paris, a team with a good scoring record (from Fig. 6b), have a tendency to perform better against more defensive teams like Atlético. Cavani, who is one of the most prolific scorers, scored in the fixture-thus validating our results. Another big fixture was the game between Juventus and Man. City in which Ronaldo scored one goal, and Dybala scored two goals. However, their efforts were in vain, as Laporte scored two headed goals off corners, and Gabriel Jesus scored one to take Manchester City to the semi-finals against Paris. Paris, being the in-form team in the semi-finals, beat Manchester City by dominating them in terms of both possession (58%) and passing

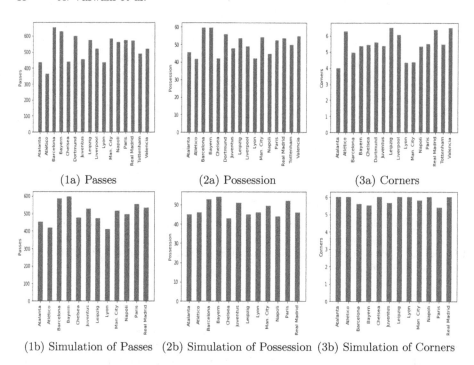

(1a) Passes   (2a) Possession   (3a) Corners

(1b) Simulation of Passes   (2b) Simulation of Possession   (3b) Simulation of Corners

Fig. 7. Distribution of Passes, Possession and Corners in training data and in our simulations. The similarity between the plots show that our model is able to learn the distribution effectively. Figure (1a) and (1b) are Passes vs Teams, Fig. (2a) and (2b) are Possession vs Teams and Fig. (3a) and (3b) are Corners vs Teams

stats, where Cavani and Peredes scored. This fixture at Manchester City's home ground was level in terms of possession(50%) and passing statistics which can be explained by Man. City's strong record at home, wherein they lost only 3 out of 18 games as seen in Fig. 1. These results validate our model's ability to learn about interactions between features.

The other semi-final was a close fixture between Bayern Munich and Barcelona. Both teams, being two of the favorites, dominated the stats at home. They established a strong home record and the match ended in a draw, with Bayern decided as winners on the basis of the highest number of shots on target (as per our chosen method). Another interesting observation was that our model could not decide the winner in this fixture over both legs, which is expected since Bayern and Barcelona were favorites to win the competition.

The final was played between Bayern Munich and Paris, where Bayern Munich emerged victorious. Few exciting observations from this simulation are discussed as follows: Lewandowski scored two goals for Bayern Munich, making a substantial contribution to Bayern's success. Bayern Munich had the highest blocks per game in the simulations, which can be explained by Manuel Neuer's brilliant performances over the last few years. Finally, the results of our model are also backed up by the fact that Bayern Munich is one of the strongest teams in the competition, and had the best form leading up to the knockout stages.

Our model can not only be used for predicting match statistics, but also for tactical analysis to help teams prepare better. We have shown that our model can make optimal predictions, and thus teams can use these predictions to be better prepared against their opposition. For example, in the simulation of a game between Bayern and Chelsea, our model predicted a significantly large number of crosses from Bayern, which matches their playing style and also reflects how a team is likely to play against another. Such analysis can help teams to plan better by focusing more on defending crosses if it is the opposition team's expected mode of attack. In addition, masked relations such as the performance of a team against relatively aggressive/defensive teams can be analysed and used to alter tactics accordingly. Finally, in order to verify the robustness of our model, we present some visualizations in Fig. 7. We show the distributions of Passes, Possession, and Corners in the training data and their distributions in predictions of our simulation. It is seen that Barcelona and Bayern lead most of these stats in the training plots, and similar distributions can be seen in the simulations. It is evident from the plots in Fig. 7 that our model is robust and can capture the information and interactions among features very well.

6   Conclusion and Future Work

Inspired by the recent focus on sports analytics, and curiosity among the community on how the current seasons would have concluded, we conducted a simulation to find out how the rest of the season would pan out. We present **UCLData**, which contains data from the UCL games between the seasons 2014-2020. We also propose a novel architecture that can efficiently capture the information and interactions within this data and make robust predictions on how individual matches of the season will pan out. We also propose solutions to handle some common problems related to data bias. Finally, we predict the results of the remaining Champions League games and thus predict the winners of this year's Champions League.

Future work can focus on giving weightage to the time of the matches, i.e. older matches will have a lower weightage as compared to the newer ones in the embedding. Although our model seems to work great on UCLData, it would be interesting to assess its learning capabilities on future football events and data from other leagues as well. Our methodology can be extended to predict other specific statistics such as the exact time of goals. Also, in the cases of a tied fixture over both legs, a penalty shootout simulation can also be added. In addition we would like to extend this work to more sporting events in the future.

References

1. Voeikov, R., Falaleev, N., Baikulov, R.: TTNet: real-time temporal and spatial video analysis of table tennis. In: Proceedings of the IEEE/CVF Conference on Computer Vision and Pattern Recognition Workshops, pp. 884–885 (2020)

2. Shih, H.: A survey of content-aware video analysis for sports. IEEE Trans. Circ. Syst. Video Technol. **28**(5), 1212–1231 (2018)
3. Rein, R., Memmert, D.: Big data and tactical analysis in elite soccer: future challenges and opportunities for sports science. SpringerPlus **5**, 12 (2016)
4. Kampakis, S., Thomas, W.: Using machine learning to predict the outcome of english county twenty over cricket matches. arXiv preprint arXiv:1511.05837 (2015)
5. Rotshtein, A.P., Posner, M., Rakityanskaya, A.B.: Football predictions based on a fuzzy model with genetic and neural tuning. Cybern. Syst. Anal. **41**(4), 619–630 (2005)
6. Joseph, A., Fenton, N.E., Neil, M.: Predicting football results using bayesian nets and other machine learning techniques. Knowl. Based Syst. **19**(7), 544–553 (2006)
7. Maystre, L., Kristof, V.: Kickoff.ai uses machine learning to predict the results of football matches (2016)
8. Maystre, L., Kristof, V., Ferrer, A.J.G., Grossglauser, M.: The player kernel: learning team strengths based on implicit player contributions. arXiv preprint arXiv:1609.01176 (2016)
9. Huang, K.Y., Chang, W.L.: A neural network method for prediction of 2006 world cup football game. In: The 2010 International Joint Conference on Neural Networks (IJCNN), pp. 1–8. IEEE (2010)
10. Hucaljuk, J., Rakipović, A.: Predicting football scores using machine learning techniques. In Proceedings of the 34th International Convention MIPRO, pp. 1623–1627. IEEE (2011)
11. Arabzad, S.M., Tayebi Araghi, M.E., Sadi-Nezhad, S., Ghofrani, N.: Football match results prediction using artificial neural networks; the case of iran pro league. J. Appl. Res. Ind. Eng. **1**(3), 159–179 (2014)
12. Flitman, A.M., Ong, E.S.: Using neural networks to predict AFL game outcomes. In IEEE Conference on Computational Intelligence and Multimedia Applications, pp. 291–295. Griffith (1997)
13. Richardson, L.: Beautiful soup documentation. April, (2007)
14. Forman, S., Kania, M.: Football statistics and history (2018). https://fbref.com/en/
15. Global sports archive. https://globalsportsarchive.com
16. Rumelhart, D.E., Hinton, G E., Williams, R.J.: Learning internal representations by error propagation. Technical report, California Univ San Diego La Jolla Inst for Cognitive Science (1985)

Physical Performance
Optimization in Football

Gergely Dobreff[1], Péter Revisnyei[1], Gábor Schuth[2], György Szigeti[2],
László Toka[1,3(✉)], and Alija Pašić[1]

[1] Budapest University of Technology and Economics, Budapest, Hungary
{dobreff,revisnyei,toka,pasic}@tmit.bme.hu
[2] Hungarian Football Federation, Budapest, Hungary
{schuth,szigeti}@mlsz.hu
[3] MTA-BME Information Systems Research Group, Budapest, Hungary

Abstract. Physical performance optimization is essential for any sport, and it is feasible in today's data-driven world. In numerous sports, it is a widely spread method to collect complex information about an athlete's performance and physiological attributes. The collected data allows to create a personalized training program to maximize the athlete's performance. Using the physiological attributes jointly with the physical load measurements can provide a refined complex picture of sportsmens', specifically football players', condition. We analyze a unique dataset that contains more than 600 key performance indicators and important physiological attributes, like the Creatine Kinase enzyme level, i.e., an indicator of muscles damage, the Heart Rate Variability that shows how well the player's heart can adapt to the exercises, and sleep quality data. We examine the relationship between the physiological factors and the physical performance of the players in training sessions and matches. We obtain the unique intervals for the relevant parameters where performance can be maximized on matchdays. After determining these optimal intervals, we introduce the Minimum Number of Training Groups (MNTG) problem in order to create the minimum number of training groups, i.e., sets of players, that can train together to maximize their performance on matchday. We find that in 96% of the time three or fewer training groups are required to optimize the performance for matchday, instead of personalized separate training for all players.

Keywords: European football · Soccer · Performance analysis · Performance optimization · Creatine kinase · Heart rate variability · Prediction

1 Introduction

Nowadays performance optimization is an essential, data-driven technique in any competitive sport: it is a widely spread method to collect complex information about the athletes' performance and physiological attributes. This is done to create a personalized training program with the ultimate goal of maximizing the athlete's performance. Using the physiological attributes besides the physical

© Springer Nature Switzerland AG 2020
U. Brefeld et al. (Eds.): MLSA 2020, CCIS 1324, pp. 51–61, 2020.
https://doi.org/10.1007/978-3-030-64912-8_5

load measurements can provide a deep understanding of the athletes' condition. Currently available wearable measurement systems provide a large amount of data suitable for data mining. The progressive trend of using all available data has also emerged in football, as it brings significant advantage against other clubs in the championship.

In this paper, we focus on how to maximize the physical performance on MatchDay (denoted as MD) by controlling the physical and physiological parameters the day before MatchDay (denoted as MD-1). Specifically, we define desired physical load intervals for MD-1 by analyzing the relationship between the used kinetic energy of the players on MD and the physical and physiological changes on MD-1. After obtaining these intervals, we introduce the Minimum Number of Training Groups (MNTG) problem, i.e., how to build the minimum number of sets of players that can train together on MD-1 to maximize their performance on MD. We have created and analyzed a unique dataset for elite youth football players. The dataset contains Creatine Kinase data (CK), Heart Rate Variability data (HRV), sleep tracking data measured with the WHOOP system (WHOOP) [21], and Player Load (PL) data measured with Catapult sports sensors [22]. Using these datasets our goal is to pinpoint relevant controllable parameters, to obtain the optimal intervals for those relevant parameters and to create the minimum number of training groups that offer the best opportunity for players to maximize their performance. This latter is achieved by solving the MNTG problem. For 96% of the training days, three or fewer training groups were sufficient instead of personalized separate training for all players. The workflow is shown in Fig. 1.

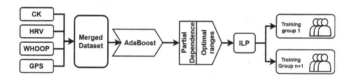

Fig. 1. The illustration of the main steps of our approach

The paper is organized as follows. In Sect. 2 we describe the background and the work related to our input data sources. In Sect. 3 we present the data preparation. In Sect. 4 we describe an Adaptive Boosting model that predicts the physical performance of each player for MD based on the physical and physiological parameters of MD-1; in addition, we apply the partial dependence method to the fitted model in order to define the optimal intervals of the parameters for each player, which we use to solve the MNTG problem in order to maximize the performance of each player on MD. In Sect. 5 we present the results of our performance and training optimization framework. Section 6 concludes the paper.

2   Data Sources and Related Work

In this section we present the background of our study. Numerous research groups have addressed the study of vital functions of athletes, examining physical and physiological parameters. The most important articles, highlighted below, are related to CK, HRV, sleep quality, and PL data. However, we emphasize that, to the best of our knowledge, such extensive research has not yet been carried out, where all these types of data were available.

2.1   Creatine Kinase Enzyme

CK is an enzyme, expressed in multiple tissues over the human body. Based on numerous studies [2,11,13,14] the increased quantity of CK enzyme in the blood indicates skeletal muscle injury. Moreover, the results of Meyer et al. [11] revealed that football-related exercises highly affect CK levels. In conclusion, during an excessive physical performance due to the occurring muscle damage, the CK level of the athlete's blood significantly elevates, i.e., a high CK level is an indicator of fatigue. Nonetheless, through the regeneration, the blood CK level will return to the baseline level. Furthermore, Osorio et al. [14] proposed that a player's biochemical profile based on the CK enzyme could help prevent muscle injuries. Consequently monitoring the CK level is crucial for estimating the muscle condition of athletes.

Our dataset contains 2062 CK datapoints, the values were measured every morning in training camps from whole blood (Reflotron Plus Clinical Chemistry Analyzer [17]) of the players.

2.2   Heart Rate Variability

HRV indicates the fluctuation of the time duration between two consecutive heartbeats, i.e., RR or NN intervals [20], which continuously changes due to the heart's adjustment to the inner and outer effects. The autonomic nervous system has the main role of affecting the heart rate trough parasympathetic and sympathetic nerve-heart interactions. According to [20], the athletes who have better endurance have a higher parasympathetic activity, thus HRV increases and the resting heart rate decreases. This study also revealed that a higher sympathetic activity on the training day causes a higher heart rate on the next day. Furthermore, the results of [10] suggest that during strenuous exercises the sympathetic nervous system dominates over the parasympathetic. In addition, [15] examined the RR intervals frequency domain in LF (Low Frequency) and HF (High Frequency) bands of basketball players, and revealed that the HRV metrics could strongly indicate the athletes' performance.

Our HRV dataset is based on RR-time curves obtained in 10-minute-long heart rate measurements while the athletes were in calm state. Our dataset contains validated metrics (SDRR (Standard deviation of RR intervals), LF, HF, HRV area) [19], based on which we can make estimations about the vegetative control of the heart, essential in terms of performance and relaxation of athletes.

2.3   Sleep Tracking

Sleeping has a crucial role in the regeneration of the body. The required amount of sleep is influenced by the time spent awake: the more time we spend awake, the more sleep is necessary for our body to regenerate properly [3]. Samuels [18] reports about multiple cases where due to existing sleeping disorders (insomnia, unsystematic sleep phases, etc.), metabolic, immunological and cognitive disorders occurred, which have a negative effect on the performance of athletes. Postolache et al. [16] highlight that in the case of younger athletes, the frequently occurring delayed sleep phase syndrome causes a decrease in the performance. Thus, those athletes who suffer from the aforementioned syndrome fall asleep hardly or not at all, hence they can not fully regenerate.

Our sleep tracking dataset was recorded by the WHOOP Strap performance monitoring device. The values describe how much time the athlete spent awake or asleep, how long the REM (Rapid Eye Movement) phase was during the sleep, etc. Because of the matches and training sessions, an athlete's body is regularly exposed to stress, thus with monitoring these metrics, we can estimate how well the athlete regenerated during the sleep.

2.4   Physical Performance

During the training sessions and matches, the Catapult system [22] was used to obtain individual physical performance data, denoted as PL data, based on its Global Positioning System receiver and microsensor, i.e., accelerometer, gyroscope, etc., information. Catapult's player equipment is a custom-made vest between the shoulder blades which does not limit the movements of arms or the torso; in the vests there are 10 Hz sensor units (Catapult S5 and G5, Catapult S7 and G7). During the study period, each player wore the same device to avoid inter-unit differences. The system simultaneously records more than 600 different performance indicators and executes further calculation to obtain derived kinetics attributes. These values reflect for each player the time spent on the field, the total distance traveled, traveled meters in a given velocity or acceleration band, and the amount of metabolic energy spent.

3   Data Preparation

Our dataset contains 2062 CK, 1347 HRV, 1335 WHOOP, and 1810 PL measurement data points. The measurements were recorded by the coaches on 27 matches over 1.5 years. All in all 48 athletes' parameters were measured on training and match days, but only 22 athletes' had sufficient data points for the proper study. In this section we present the data preparation steps we took.

3.1   Joining and Filtering

The four data sources described in Sect. 2 provides a unique dataset and opportunity for analyzing the performance of elite youth football players. First, we have to combine those into one dataset to store the player's CK, HRV, WHOOP, and PL data on given days. To investigate how a player's physical performance on MD is affected by the MD-1 workload and physiological data, we select the players who played on given MDs. Then for those players we select the CK and HRV in the morning of MD-1, the MD-1 WHOOP and PL data, and we add the MD morning CK level and HRV data, and the metabolic energy [KJ/kg] of the PL data during the match. The latter is the total energy consumption per unit mass, which plays a key role in the calculation of physical performance in a match. With these steps, we have created a dataset where each row includes the player ID, the match performance of a given player, CK and HRV measurements on MD, and CK, HRV, WHOOP and training session PL measurements of MD-1. The dataset contains 314 data points from 22 players.

3.2   Handling Missing Values

Unfortunately almost 5.75% of all the data were missing data. These were handled by the following techniques.

- **CK:** The correlation between the CK level measured in the morning of MD and of MD-1 is significant. Using the findings of Kobayashi et al. [8], which state that strenuous exercise produces beneficial changes in lipid blood profiles, we utilize PL and CK data to construct personalized models to fill in the missing values. Linear models are used - as they seem to be the best performing models - to capture the individual characteristics. According to the Kolmogorov-Smirnov test, the distribution of CK does not change significantly with the filled data (p-value > 0.99, where the significance level is 0.05): from 395.3 ± 258.0 to 395.2 ± 254.5.
- **HRV:** On some MDs and training days some players' HRV was not measured. According to Hedelin et al. [5], the performance, i.e., peak torque and total work, and the HRV show strong relationship. Therefore we can infer the HRV using the PL data. We built personalized models with Random Forest Regressors [6] since authors of [5] state that non-linear relationships exist. We examined all 37 HRV attributes and we can state that their distributions do not change significantly according to Kolmogorov-Smirnov tests (with p-value > 0.5, where the significance level is 0.05).
- **WHOOP:** By examining sleep data we determine that the sleep patterns are unique and consistent, i.e., the sleep of a particular player is usually of the same quality. Sleep resting heart rate (RHR), HRV, deep sleep duration, and REM phase lengths may vary from person to person, but by player these show similar values. We find that the RHR and HRV of the player during sleep and the proportion of length of deep sleep and REM phase to the total sleep are always within a well-defined range. In addition, this behavior also appears to be independent of being collected during a pre-match or a pre-training sleep. To fill in the missing values, we calculated the mean and standard deviation of each player's sleep parameters. The missing data are then replaced by randomly selected values around the mean, thus the distribution of values is not significantly affected. Note that due to the strict sleeping schedule in training camps, the variance in sleep tracking data of the players is usually rather low.

4   Exploring the Dataset

After the data preparation we create machine learning models which can explore the relationships between the variables. Utilizing the fitted models we define for each variable the optimal intervals in which players maximize their performance on MD. We use this information to create appropriate training groups.

4.1   Modelling Methods

Our goal is to explore the relationship between MD-1 training sessions and MD performance with machine learning models. We use the *metabolic energy of MD divided by the time spent on the field* (denoted as M_t) metric as the target variable. This shows total energy consumption per unit mass of the players and since it is divided by the play time, it is comparable even if players did not spend the same amount of time on the pitch. We use all the attributes measured on MD-1 as predictor variables. The last 20% of the dataset forms the test set. The building of the models is performed on the train set which includes the following steps: first, we define the key variables with feature selection methods, second, with the selected features we build multiple models and select the best one. These steps are discussed in details in the rest of this section.

Feature Selection. We describe the physical and physiological condition of the players with 651 different attributes. To create the best possible machine learning model to predict the target variable, we have to select those metrics which contain the most relevant information. The merged dataset includes redundant and irrelevant metrics which can be omitted from the dataset and hence reduce the number of dimensions to avoid the "curse of dimensionality" [1]. In order to make a comprehensive selection, each of the following three methodologies results in a set of potentially good feature sets. The union of them is used later for building the model. In the first approach, we select the metrics which have higher correlation with the target variable than a certain threshold (0.8). All others are omitted. However, among the selected variables redundant variable pairs might occur, so to omit such variables we analyze the cross-correlation and if necessary, we omit one of them. For our second approach, we utilize existing algorithms from the review article of Li et al. [9] that were developed for feature selection: Fischer score, Laplacian score, Spectral feature selection, Unsupervised discriminative feature selection. In the third approach, we take advantage of the fact that some machine learning models perform feature selection while learning, e.g., the Lasso Regression and the Gradient Boosting Machine. The Lasso method omits features that are not relevant, hence creating a potentially good feature set. Decision trees built by Gradient Boosting Machine can be examined to determine which attributes are important in predicting the target variable.

Building the Models. We build machine learning models for each player separately using the previously discussed feature selection methods in order to explore potential relationships between the variables. As we perform a regression analysis, we select the Root Mean Squared Error (RMSE) to evaluate the models. We use 4-fold cross-validation in order to select the best feature set and the hyper-parameters for the models and to estimate the capabilities of the model as precisely as possible. We examine the following models: Lasso Regression, Ridge Regression, Elastic Net, Gradient Boosting Machine and AdaBoost. The first three linear models perform badly compared to Gradient Boosting Machine and AdaBoost. The model parameters are fine-tuned by exhaustive search. The optimal value of the hyperparameters of the best performing model (AdaBoost) was searched in the following ranges: 10–500 number of trees, 0.01-0.1 learning rate and the max depth of the trees 2–8. Table 1 shows the overall results of the mentioned models.

Table 1. The results of the models.

Model Name	RMSE	R^2 value
Ridge regression	0.000152	0.784
Lasso regression	0.000140	0.816
ElasticNet	0.000134	0.831
AdaBoost	0.000128	0.846
Gradient Boosting Machine	0.000133	0.831

According to the results in Table 1, the best approach is to use the AdaBoost model (RMSE: 0.000128, R^2: 0.846) for each player individually with features that describe the MD morning CK level, the MD-1 training session's maximum heart rate, micro movements with high acceleration and the given velocity target bands of the players. Note that we examined the possibility of omitting data imputation as described in Sect. 3.2 since AdaBoost can automatically handle the missing values. However, in this case only an RMSE of 0.000168 was achieved.

We examined the potential of a player agnostic model, i.e., one model for the entire team, and forming player clusters (based on the physiological attributes) to design more robust models, however, they did not yield better results.

4.2   Optimal Intervals of Physiological and Physical Values

In order to determine the optimal intervals of physiological values on MD-1 morning and that of the optimal physical values in the MD-1 training for each player, we utilize the Partial Dependence [12] method. This method reveals the effect of each attribute on the value predicted by the given machine learning model, i.e., shows the relationship between the target variable of the model (in our case the player's metabolic energy divided by the field time i.e., M_t) and the selected attribute. Using the partial dependence diagrams, we determine the optimal range of values: if the players' attributes fall within these intervals on MD-1, it follows that the value of the target variable will be maximized. An example for such intervals are the following: MD morning CK 204 ± 91 to 667 ± 199, max heart rate 131 ± 55 to 180 ± 41 and number of micro movements with high acceleration 4 ± 2 to 29 ± 12. The details of the predictive model for the CK levels in the morning of MD based on those of the morning of MD-1 and the training PL of MD-1 are omitted from this manuscript due to page limits.

The optimal intervals defined on CK, HRV and PL type variables are further used to form the minimum number of training groups on MD-1 to maximize the performance on MD for each player. We highlight that according to the feature selection there are no relevant sleep tracking data (WHOOP) intervals, this is due to the fact that the training camps are very controlled environment, thus the data exhibits low variance.

4.3   Solving MNTG Using Graph Coloring

We define the Minimum Number of Training Groups problem (MNTG), in which the goal is to create training groups so that each player would get into their optimal range, with and as few training groups as possible. Hence we define training sessions in such a manner that players are able to participate in the same training session - according to our conditions - only if the optimal intervals of their attributes intersect. The fact that one player can participate in a training session with another player can be represented as a graph G, with nodes representing players and edges representing the fact that two given players can participate in the same training session. Consequently we can formulate our problem by looking for the minimum number of (distinct) cliques which can cover G, thus we are looking for a minimal clique cover for G. So in the complement graph of G, we need to find a minimum vertex coloring [7]. This can be done by well known ILP algorithms [4]. By solving the ILP, the vertices of the same color found in the complement of G represent the cliques in G, which in our case denote the training sessions and the players involved, the solution to the MNTG problem.

5   Results

We have been able to identify the parameters that must be considered when planning pre-match training sessions. We have individually determined the ranges of physiological parameters, in which players can maximize physical performance on matchdays, so we set out to plan their prior workouts accordingly. Our intent then was to create the best training session for our players with the least amount of resources, e.g., personal trainers. The examined 22 players participated in 27 matches, and since players' CK levels vary between matches, the optimal training groups, i.e., the solution of MNTG, have to be determined before each MD.

Table 2 shows an example of our results: we determine which players should have trained together (e.g. Players 1, 3, 5 in Case 1) and who required regeneration, e.g., Players 1, 5 in Case 3) before the match, i.e., on an MD-1.

Table 2. Training groups of different MD-1 days (from Cases 1 to 7). A, B, C are different training groups, Reg. means the player required a regeneration training and N.P. means the player was not present that day.

	Case 1	Case 2	Case 3	Case 4	Case 5	Case 6	Case 7
Player 1	B	A	Reg.	N.P.	B	N.P.	B
Player 2	C	B	C	N.P.	C	A	C
Player 3	B	A	C	C	B	A	B
Player 4	C	B	C	C	C	A	C
Player 5	A	Reg.	A	A	A	N.P.	A

Our results confirmed that players require different training sessions according to body type and player position. The professional staff confirmed that the individual differences were apparent in our training groups. Some interesting results are the following. Four players who are grouped together in most of the training sessions, all lack explosivity. This can be seen in the data: they require 17% longer runs in the low speed band and 6% less runs in the high speed band than the others. One of the players has demanded several regeneration training sessions (8 to be exact), because he is extremely sensitive to high loads, so his CK levels easily increase dramatically. His optimal range for the MD morning CK is $444 - 850$ while it is $165 - 675$ for others. Two other players needed regeneration training sessions due to minor injuries, the presence of which was evident in the extreme elevation in their CK levels. The goalkeeper always trains alone.

According to our results, 4% of training days did not require regeneration training and players could be trained in two separate groups. Five groups and a regeneration group was required in 4% of the cases. On the rest of the MD-1 days, 2 (30%) and 3 (62%) groups were sufficient along with the regeneration training, i.e., in 96% of the time three or fewer training groups are required to optimize the performance for MD, which means there is no need for dividing players into smaller groups. Note that, surprisingly 4 training groups were not necessary in any case.

As a result of our work, we have created a framework for optimizing the matchday performance according to the physiological measurements on the prior day. The customized training is given to control those parameters into their optimal interval, greatly facilitating the work of the trainers.

6   Conclusion

In our paper, we examined the relationship between the physiological factors and the physical performance of the players in training sessions and matches. We obtained the optimal intervals for the relevant parameters to optimize the physical performance on matchday. After obtaining the optimal load intervals, we showed our solution to the MNTG problem i.e., how to obtain the minimum number of sets of players that can train together before the matchday to optimize their performance on matchday. We showed that in 96% of pre-match days three or fewer training groups are required to optimize the performance for the match, which means there is no need for training players individually or in small groups.

Acknowledgement. This work was supported by the National Research, Development and Innovation Office of Hungary (NKFIH) in research project FK 128233, financed under the FK_18 funding scheme.

References

1. Bellman, R.: Dynamic programming treatment of the travelling salesman problem. J. ACM **9**(1), 61–63 (1962)
2. Brancaccio, P., Maffulli, N., Limongelli, F.M.: Creatine kinase monitoring in sport medicine. Br. Med. Bull. **81**(1), 209–230 (2007)
3. Dijk, D.J., Lockley, S.W.: Invited review: integration of human sleep-wake regulation and circadian rhythmicity. J. Appl. Physiol. **92**(2), 852–862 (2002)
4. Faigle, U., Kern, W., Still, G.: Algorithmic Principles of Mathematical Programming. chap. 9, pp. 181–182, Springer Science & Business Media (2013)
5. Hedelin, R., Bjerle, P., Henriksson-Larsen, K.: Heart rate variability in athletes: relationship with central and peripheral performance. Med. Sci. Sports Exercise **33**(8), 1394–1398 (2001)
6. Ho, T.K.: Random decision forests. In: Proceedings of 3rd International Conference on Document Analysis and Recognition, vol. 1, pp. 278–282. IEEE (1995)
7. Karp, R.M.: Reducibility among combinatorial problems. In: Complexity of Computer Computations. The IBM Research Symposia Series. Springer, Boston, MA (1972)
8. Kobayashi, Y., Takeuchi, T., Hosoi, T., Yoshizaki, H., Loeppky, J.A.: Effect of a marathon run on serum lipoproteins, creatine kinase, and lactate dehydrogenase in recreational runners. Res. Q. Exerc. Sport **76**(4), 450–455 (2005)
9. Li, J., et al.: Feature selection: a data perspective. ACM Comput. Surv. **50**(6), 1–45 (2017)
10. Maciel, B., Gallo, J.L., Marin, J.N., Lima, E.F., Martins, L.: Autonomic nervous control of the heart rate during dynamic exercise in normal man. Clin. Sci. **71**(4), 457–460 (1986)
11. Meyer, T., Meister, S.: Routine blood parameters in elite soccer players. Int. J. Sports Med. **32**(11), 875–881 (2011)
12. Molnar, C.: Interpretable Machine Learning. Lulu.com (2019)
13. Mougios, V.: Reference intervals for serum creatine kinase in athletes. Br. J. Sports Med. **41**(10), 674–678 (2007)
14. Osorio, J.J., Méndez, E.A., Aguirre-Acevedo, D., Osorio-Ciro, J., Calderón, J.C., Gallo-Villegas, J.A.: Creatine phosphokinase and urea asbiochemical markers of muscle injuries in professional football players. Asian J. Sports Med. **9**(4) (2018)
15. Paul, M., Garg, K.: The effect of heart rate variability biofeedback on performance psychology of basketball players. Appl. Psychophysiol. Biofeedback **37**(2), 131–144 (2012)
16. Postolache, T.T., Hung, T.M., Rosenthal, R.N., Soriano, J.J., Montes, F., Stiller, J.W.: Sports chronobiology consultation: from the lab to the arena. Clin. Sports Med. **24**(2), 415–456 (2005)

17. Roche, Mannheim, Germany: Reflotron plus clinical chemistry analyzer, https:// diagnostics.roche.com
18. Samuels, C.: Sleep, recovery, and performance: the new frontier in high-performance athletics. Neurol. Clin. **26**(1), 169–180 (2008)
19. Shaffer, F., Ginsberg, J.: An overview of heart rate variability metrics and norms. Frontiers Public Health **5**, 258 (2017)
20. Vanderlei, L.C.M., Pastre, C.M., Hoshi, R.A., Carvalho, T.D.D., Godoy, M.F.D.: Basic notions of heart rate variability and its clinical applicability. Braz. J. Cardiovasc. Surg. **24**(2), 205–217 (2009)
21. WHOOP: Whoop strap 3.0. https://www.whoop.com/
22. Catapult Group International Ltd. https://www.catapultsports.com/

Predicting Player Trajectories in Shot Situations in Soccer

Per Lindström[1,2], Ludwig Jacobsson[2], Niklas Carlsson[1],
and Patrick Lambrix[1(✉)]

[1] Linköping University, Linköping, Sweden
{niklas.carlsson,patrick.lambrix}@liu.se
[2] Signality, Linköping, Sweden
https://www.signality.com/

Abstract. Player behaviors can have a significant impact on the outcome of individual events, as well as the game itself. The increased availability of high quality resolution spatio-temporal data has enabled analysis of player behavior and game strategy. In this paper, we present the implementation and evaluation of an imitation learning method using recurrent neural networks, which allows us to learn individual player behaviors and perform rollouts of player movements on previously unseen play sequences. The method is evaluated using a 2019 dataset from the top-tier soccer league in Sweden (Allsvenskan). Our evaluation provides insights how to best apply the method on movement traces in soccer, the relative accuracy of the method, and how well policies of one player role capture the relative behaviors of a different player role, for example.

1 Introduction

In recent years the availability of tracking data has grown considerably, through the use of wearable GPS trackers and advances in optical object tracking. This has made it possible for analysts to provide deeper insights than before. For example, in soccer, work has been done on such issues as player and team analysis [2,3], player ghosting [26], and predicting ball position [23].

An important factor that can be learned from this data is player movement. Once we can learn and predict player movement, interesting questions can be asked and answered. For instance, one may obtain insights on a particular player's movement patterns in a particular situation and thereby have a better chance to find strategies to counter that player. It may also be possible to find players that have similar patterns and may therefore be seen as possible substitutes for one another. By substituting the patterns of two players it may also be possible to see how different players act in and solve different game situations. Comparing a player to a league average player or to a league average player with a certain role, may give insights on a player's creativity, but could also be used in training to show a player when good or bad decisions are made. Further, defensive and offensive effectiveness in different situations may be investigated.

© Springer Nature Switzerland AG 2020
U. Brefeld et al. (Eds.): MLSA 2020, CCIS 1324, pp. 62–75, 2020.
https://doi.org/10.1007/978-3-030-64912-8_6

In this paper we present a method to predict player movement based on imitation learning (Sect. 4). Through experiments (Sect. 5) we give technical insights as well as validation and player comparisons. The method is evaluated using a 2019 dataset from the top-tier soccer league in Sweden (Allsvenskan). Our results highlight how to best apply the method on movement traces from soccer so to achieve good accuracy, validate the accuracy of the models (e.g., as function of time since rollout starts and player role), and provide insights regarding how well different player-specific policies (learned using our model) capture the relative behaviors of different player roles (e.g., similarities and differences between different player roles) and illustrate how different player behaviors can be compared with the use of rollout using different player profiles.

2   Related Work

In many sports (but for the sake of brevity we focus on soccer), work has started on game play. For instance, in soccer, there is work on rating actions [9,36], pass prediction [5,7,15,21,39], shot prediction [29], expectation for goals given a game state [8] or a possession [11], or more general game strategies [1,4,12, 14,16,17,28]. Game play information can be used to predict the outcome of a game by estimating the probability of scoring for the individual goal scoring opportunities [10], by relating games to the players in the teams [30], or by using team rating systems [24]. It can also be used to measure player performance by investigating in metrics [37], skills [22,31,40,41], performance under pressure [6] and on the correlation with market value [18]. Tracking data is used for player and team analysis [2,3], game analysis [13], and predicting ball position [23]. An interactive system allowing for querying and analyzing tracking data is described in [38]. The work closest related to ours is [26,27] where imitation learning is used to learn the general behavior of inferred roles or in a multi-agent setting. In our work we use imitation learning to learn the behavior of specific players.

3   Background

In this work we use two learning phases each using a version of imitation learning. In imitation learning (e.g., [32]) a *policy* π is trained to imitate the behavior of an expert. The setting for the learning contains *states* representing what an agent perceives at a given time step, and *actions*, that allow us to go from one state to another. The expert π^* generates the observed state-action pairs which the learned policy should imitate. In the first phase we use behavioral cloning (e.g., [35]), where the policy maps states to actions. In the second phase we learn a policy that maps a state and a set of contexts to a *trajectory with horizon* T which consists of a set of T states (and actions). The latter mapping is also called a *rollout*, and is achieved by sequentially executing π given an initial state. Two distributions of states are used to train the policies. A distribution of states visited by the expert is defined as $P^* = P(x|\pi^*)$, while a distribution of states induced by policy π_θ, parameterized by θ, is given by $P(x|\theta)$.

The distribution P^* is provided from observations of the expert and the cost is given by $C(\pi^*(x), \pi(x))$. As it may not be possible to know or observe the true cost function for a task, a surrogate loss ℓ, is adopted, which can be minimized instead of C. The learning goal for behavioral cloning (first phase) is then to find the parameters, which make the policy imitate the expert with minimal surrogate loss. The best policy $\hat{\pi}_\theta$ is then given by $\hat{\pi}_\theta = \operatorname{argmin}_\theta \mathbb{E}_{x \sim P^*} \ell(\pi^*(x), \pi_\theta(x))$. In general imitation learning (second phase), the distribution of states is instead given by rollouts and the best policy is $\hat{\pi}_\theta = \operatorname{argmin}_\theta \mathbb{E}_{x \sim P(s|\theta)} \ell(\pi^*(x), \pi_\theta(x))$.

4 Approach

Model. In our setting the expert in the imitation learning is a soccer player that we want to model. A state $x \equiv (s, c)$ is comprised of two parts: the system state s describing the modelled player, and the context c describing all other players and the ball. In our work a state is represented by a state vector. For each entity in a state, i.e., all players on the field and the ball, we store the position on the field as Cartesian coordinates. The entities in each state are sorted so that their order in the state is consistent over the duration of a sequence. This is needed for learning and interpreting changes of an entity over time. The players in each state are grouped per team, and within their team they are sorted according to their lineup index provided by the league. Lineup indices are consistent through games, and thus also consistent through any subsequence within a game. The modelled player p_m, is placed at the beginning of the state vector. This is done in order to explicitly show the model which player that is being modelled, since its position in the lineup may differ between games. p_m is followed by all players in his team, all players in the opponent team and finally the ball. Further, an action in a state results in a change in position.

The policies used in our experiments are implemented in Keras (https://keras.io/) as multi-variable regression models. Given a state x_t where t represents the order in a sequence of states, a policy π predicts an action $\hat{a}_t = \pi(x_t)$ which describes how p_m's position has changed in $t + 1$. When a policy predicts an action $\hat{a}_t$ on state x_t, it receives as input a sequence of state vectors representing states $x_{t-w}, ..., x_t$. This sequence can be thought of as the memory of the model, as information from the states in this sequence can be used for deciding on the prediction of the action. The size w of this sequence is called the *window*. Our model is implemented using a Long Short-Term Memory (LSTM) network with two LSTM layers with 512 nodes in each layer (similar to [26,27]). The model has a total of 3,253,250 trainable parameters.

Sequences are rolled out by feeding consecutive states into a policy and iteratively making predictions on those while updating the next system state given the current action. The predicted sequence $\hat{X}$ is initiated with the first w state vectors of the observed sequence X: $\hat{X}_{0:w} = X_{0:w}$ The predicted sequence $\hat{X}$ can then be rolled out by predicting an action $\hat{a}_t = \pi(\hat{x}_t)$ using $\{\hat{x}_{t-w}..., \hat{x}_t\}$. The following system state s_{t+1} in $\hat{x}_{t+1}$ is updated with the result of $\hat{a}_t$. This process is applied iteratively on each $\hat{x} \in \hat{X}$, from $t = w$ to $t = T$, where T

is the horizon. Each state is updated with the predicted action, which means that any deviation (or error) introduced by the policy is propagated through the sequence. A policy π is evaluated by rolling it out on a set of sequences S over a horizon of T time steps. During the rollout of each sequence X, the Euclidean distance d_t between p_m's position in x_t and $\hat{x}_t$ is calculated for each time step t. The distance d_t is referred to as the *error*. The mean error at t for a set of sequences S can be obtained by averaging the errors for all sequences in S at time step t. The global error is calculated by averaging the mean errors for all time steps in a rollout.

Algorithm 1. Sequence training

Input: Training sequences $\mathcal{S}_{tr}$, Validation sequences $\mathcal{S}_v$,
Input: Pre-trained policy π_0,
Input: Training horizon T_h, Epochs N
Output: Policy π
  1: $\mathcal{D} \leftarrow \emptyset$
  2: $\mathcal{S}_0 \leftarrow \mathcal{S}_{tr}$
  3: **for** $j = 1$ **to** T_h **do**
  4:      $\mathcal{S}_j \leftarrow \mathcal{S}_{j-1}$
  5:      **for** $X = \{x_0, ..., x_T\}$ **in** $\mathcal{S}_{j-1}$ **do**
  6:          **for** $t = 0$ **to** $T_h - 1$ **do**
  7:              Predict $\hat{a}_t = \pi_0(x_t)$
  8:              Calculate $\hat{x}_{t+1} = \texttt{calculate\_state}(\hat{a}_t, x_t, x_{t+1})$
  9:              Add $(\hat{x}_{t+1}, a_{t+1})$ to $\mathcal{D}$
10:              Replace x_{t+1} in X with the generated state $\hat{x}_{t+1}$
11: **for** $i = 1$ **to** N **do**
12:      $\pi_i \leftarrow \pi_{i-1}$
13:      Train π_i on $\mathcal{D}$
14:      Validate π_i on $\mathcal{S}_v$
15: **return** Best π_i on sequence validation loss

Learning. The training process is divided into two phases. During both phases, mean squared error is adopted to calculate loss. In the first phase the policy is pre-trained on state-action pairs from training sequences. This is classical supervised learning and teaches the policy the mapping from observed states x_t to expert actions a_t. The policy is trained during N epochs and the best policy is returned, based on validation loss. The validation data $\mathcal{D}_v$ is made up of all state-action pairs from the validation sequences. In the second phase the policy is trained on (partially) rolled out sequences as described in Algorithm 1. The approach is based on DAgger [33] and the imitation learning algorithms used in [26,27]. In the first part of the algorithm (lines 3–10) the set of training data from the first phase is augmented by (partially) rolling out those sequences. This is done by using the pre-trained policy π_0 to gradually make one-step predictions on each time step t in each sequence X of the training sequences $\mathcal{S}_{tr}$, adding all generated state-action pairs to a new dataset $\mathcal{D}$, and then iterating

Table 1. Summary of dataset.

Season	Period	Games	Players	Events	Goals	Other shots
2019	March 31–June 2	79	276	1,668	193	1,475

over the sequences again with the states generated in the last round. This process is performed T_h times as specified by the training horizon parameter. The training horizon should be lower or equal than the sequence horizon; $T_h \leq T$. The *calculate_state* function on line 8 calculates a predicted state $\hat{x}_{t+1}$ where the system state of $\hat{x}_{t+1}$ is based on the current system state s_t and action $\hat{a}_t$, and the context of $\hat{x}_{t+1}$ is the context c_{t+1} of x_{t+1}.

In the second part (lines 11–14) the policy is trained on this augmented data set and validated by rolling out on full sequences in a validation set using their global errors as validation loss. Finally, the best policy is returned based on sequence validation loss, which is the global error given by rolling out on the validation sequences. Although many single-agent imitation learning applications use dynamic oracles [27,33] to generate one-step corrections a_t^* for each sampled state $\hat{x}_t$, dynamic oracles are expensive and require complex training schemas, and there has been research on circumventing the need for dynamic oracles when learning to roll out sequences [19,25]. Algorithm 1 follows their example by using the observed expert demonstrations to teach the policy how to behave in the sampled states.

5   Experiments

5.1   Data and Data Preparation

Data. The dataset used in this paper was provided by Signality, a startup company that delivers sports analytics for customers such as the top-tier soccer league in Sweden. The dataset captures all 79 games played before the summer break of the 2019 season, and includes tracking data, game metadata, and manually annotated event data. The tracking was created by applying Signality's automated object detection and recognition technology on game video recordings. The tracking data has a sample rate of 25 Hz and contained trajectories of all players and the ball. Each trajectory contains position, speed and a trajectory identifier at every time step. All positions are represented by Cartesian coordinates $(x, y) \in [0, 1] \times [0, 1]$. Each trajectory is assigned a jersey number as soon as it is recognized by the system. The tracking data also contains basic statistics such as each player's accumulated distance, passes and ball possession. The game metadata includes information such as arena information, pitch size, and team lineup, as well as information about the players and teams in the game. This data is used to create a mapping from trajectory identifiers to player identities, roles and lineup. The manually annotated data contains game events such as shots, yellow cards, medical treatment, substitutions, and goals.

These events are used to, e.g., find sequences of interest to train and evaluate policies. We preprocessed the data by padding missing values or entities with the value -1, by scaling the coordinates to the size of an average Swedish soccer pitch ($105 \times 64\,\text{m}^2$), and downsampling the sample rate to $5\,\text{Hz}$, or one frame per $200\,\text{ms}$.

Training and Validation Data. In this paper we focus on situations related to goals and shots. The training and validation data are therefore sequences related to such situations. We extracted sequences starting $10\,\text{s}$ before and ending $10\,\text{s}$ after an annotated shot, and for which each state in the sequence contains the observed coordinates for p_m. Each sequence contains up to 100 observed states. The modelled team can either be the defending team or the attacking team in the extracted sequences. Table 1 summarizes the key characteristics associated with the dataset. For the analysis presented here, we focus on the 150 players (out of 276) with the most games (in this case 12–24 games per player). From the 1,668 annotated events, play sequences for the 150 players were added randomly to both the training and validation dataset. For the training dataset, we extracted randomly two sequences from each game half (when at least three annotated sequences existed) and assigned the rest of the sequences to the training set. (When only two sequences existed, one was assigned for the evaluation, and when only one existed it was only used for training.) In total, 5,188 random sequences were used for validation and 21,284 sequences were used for training. All arenas and lineups are represented during both training and validation.

Visualization. To reason regarding the behavior of a policy, rollouts are visualized as plots on a soccer pitch. Each dot is one observed data point. The spacing between each dot in a trajectory is $200\,\text{ms}$. Yellow dots are the ground truth, or the observed player trajectory. Turquoise dots are the rolled out policy, with the first dot coinciding with the player's actual initial state. The big dot of a trajectory shows the final position of that player. Red and blue dots represent positions of the other players, and white dots observed ball positions.

5.2   Technical Evaluation Insights

The calculations are resource intensive and take time. For this reason, we use limited player samples to first determining a promising learning methodology. Here, we highlight the insights obtained from three such steps.

Absolute vs. Relative Actions. Actions can be represented using absolute actions, i.e, using the coordinates of consecutive player positions (e.g., [26]), or relative actions, i.e, using the difference between the consecutive positions (e.g., [34]). We investigate the influence of the representation on the learned policy. For these experiments, we used five random players, and each policy was trained for each action type and player. For both training and validation we used a window size of 20 time steps. Over the 9,500 samples associated with these players the absolute method had an average error of $9.01\,\text{m}$ with a standard deviation of $7.22\,\text{m}$. The corresponding error using the relative method

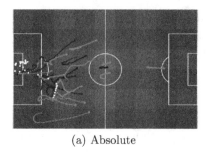   

(a) Absolute   (b) Relative

Fig. 1. Example rollouts.

was 6.89 m (σ = 5.84 m). We note these values (both averages and standard variations) are smaller, that the 95% confidence intervals (i.e., [8.87, 9.16] and [6.77, 7.01]) are non-overlapping, and that the null hypothesis that the average errors are the same can be rejected with a t-score of 22.25 (>1.96). In general, we have found that the relative actions also result in smoother rollout behavior from the start. This is illustrated in Fig. 1, which shows example rollouts using the two methods. Motivated by the smaller errors and smoother rollouts, in the following experiments, we use only the relative actions.

We note that [26] has shown that it is possible to get smooth results with absolute actions, and we may be able to obtain this with other parameters, an extended state description, or more data. Further, a drawback of using relative actions without a dynamic oracle [27] is that the policy is taught to move in the same direction that the expert did in a certain time step even if it during the rollout in sequence training has deviated significantly from the original trajectory.

Baseline Comparisons. We note that our methodology differs from most prior work on imitation learning in that we circumvent the need for dynamic oracles when learning to roll out sequences. While this still allows us to imitate the general behavior of players, this naturally results in the absolute positional error increasing over time. To put these errors in perspective, we compared the learned policies with policies generated using a random walk algorithm (providing a kind of upper bound) and the results obtained when evaluating the policies on the training data itself (providing a kind of rough lower bound). For this analysis we used the same set of five players as above. For the random walk, random steps were sampled from a normal distribution specified by the mean and standard deviation of movement observed in the dataset. With these settings, we obtained a global error of 10.17 m (random walk) and 4.75 m (training, relative actions), respectively. Despite a relatively unfair comparison, these results suggest that our relative action approach shows promising results in that it has errors closer to what the policy achieves on the training data itself than a random walk. Trajectories that are confined to a small area naturally exhibit lower errors for the random walk, while the opposite is true for longer trajectories. Furthermore, although the difference in global error for the learned policy and the random

Table 2. Impact of window size.

Window	Mean	Stdev	Conf interval
10	7.60	6.23	[7.47, 7.73]
20	7.14	5.70	[7.02, 7.26]
30	7.42	6.05	[7.30, 7.55]
40	7.72	6.04	[7.60, 7.85]
50	7.23	6.30	[7.10, 7.36]

walk policy is not that high, a qualitative assessment of the rollouts makes it clear that for the random walk the rollouts are random, and the policy does not follow the general movement of the sequence at all, whereas the method presented here does (e.g., Fig. 1).

Window Size. To investigate the influence of the window size, multiple policies were trained with variations on this parameter. The window size limits the policy's memory and gives an upper bound on the longest time frame for retained information. Further, from a performance perspective, longer window sizes require more computation during training and prediction [20]. Table 2 shows example results for five different window sizes. Interestingly, we have observed the highest accuracy with an intermediate window size of 20 time steps (our default window). While the relative errors for different window sizes are relatively similar, the window size of 20 time steps results in somewhat smaller averages than the other window sizes (statistically significant at the 95% confidence level compared to all windows except 50). It is also interesting to note that both the averages and the standard deviations are smallest for these intermediate window sizes. These results suggest that the policies are not able to fully utilize the additional information captured by the larger window sizes. In the following, we use a window size of 20 time steps.

Multi-player-Based pre-Training. We have observed significant value using multi-player based pre-training. To illustrate this, here we present evaluation results showing how pre-training on other players' observations compares to only pre-training on player p_m's observations, in terms of rollout error on validation sequences from p_m. For these experiments, we used five (new) random players and trained the modeled players using only data for the player itself (as in the prior experiments presented in this section) or using data for all players, respectively. To avoid influence of goalkeepers (who have much different movement patterns), we only used data for non-goalkeepers here. Again, we use a window size of 20 time steps and evaluate over 50 time steps, and use the relative actions. When only pre-training using the player itself we obtain an error of 7.12 m ($\sigma = 5.96$ m), and when using pre-training using multiple players we obtain an error of 6.73 m ($\sigma = 5.59$ m). Over 7,800 samples, this results in non-overlapping confidence intervals (i.e., [6.99, 7.25] vs. [6.61, 6.85]) and a t-value of 4.22 (>1.96).

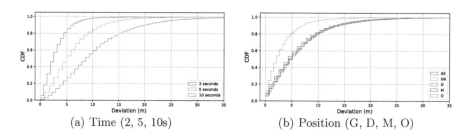

(a) Time (2, 5, 10s)   (b) Position (G, D, M, O)

Fig. 2. CDFs of the relative errors.

Table 3. Error for different player roles.

Position	Mean (stdev)	Players	Samples
Goalkeepers (G)	3.30 (3.30)	13	25,700
Defensive (D)	6.49 (5.69)	63	108,300
Midfielder (M)	6.69 (6.07)	45	76,350
Offensive (O)	6.71 (6.05)	29	49,050

5.3 Validation and Player Comparisons

Motivated by the above findings, in the remainder we use the relative actions, a 20 time step window, and multi-player pre-training for our learning and evaluation. For this section, we present results over all 150 players. Overall, over the 259,400 samples considered we observe an average error of 6.27 m ($\sigma = 5.77$ m).

Error Accumulation. Figure 2(a) shows the Cumulative Distribution Function (CDF) distributions of the error in the absolute player position after 2, 5, or 10 s have elapsed. It should be noted that the shots typically happen 6–8 s into the sequences, and can cause significant changes in players' actions on the pitch. For this reason, it is perhaps not surprising that the tail of the distribution (with larger errors) increases significantly between the 5 s and 10 s time stamps.

Player Role Breakdown. In general, we have observed similar prediction errors for all categories except goalkeepers. This is illustrated by the tight clustering of the other categories (D, M, O) CDFs in Fig. 2(b), but can also be seen from looking at the average errors of the different categories (Table 3). Here, the defender (D) category includes all "backs", (M) includes "midfielders", and the offensive (O) category includes "forwards" or "wings" as annotated by Allsvenskan.

Direction Errors. Despite the model targeting general behavior, rather then definite prediction, we have found that it often does a reasonable job predicting the direction of the player movement. Here, we present prediction results for the general direction, as defined by in which out of four directions the player moves the furthest: forward (i.e., towards the opposition's end), backwards, inwards (i.e., towards the middle of the field), or outwards. These general directions are

Table 4. Confusion matrix for directional prediction errors over 2 s, 5 s, and 10 s.

		Predictions						Predictions						Predictions		
		In	Out	Fwd	Bkwd			In	Out	Fwd	Bkwd			In	Out	Fwd	Bkwd
Truth	In	**0.24**	0.20	0.29	0.27	Truth	In	**0.26**	0.18	0.30	0.26	Truth	In	**0.20**	0.20	0.30	0.30
	Out	0.08	**0.39**	0.26	0.27		Out	0.08	**0.42**	0.25	0.25		Out	0.07	**0.46**	0.24	0.23
	Fwd	0.09	0.16	**0.67**	0.08		Fwd	0.09	0.19	**0.62**	0.10		Fwd	0.09	0.19	**0.64**	0.09
	Bkwd	0.09	0.20	0.08	**0.62**		Bkwd	0.09	0.21	0.09	**0.62**		Bkwd	0.09	0.19	0.10	**0.62**

(a) 2 s (F1=0.53)   (b) 5 s (F1=0.52)   (c) 10 s (F1=0.53)

Table 5. Cross-evaluation using ten random players - errors.

		Observed expert player									
		G1	D1	D2	D3	D4	M1	M2	M3	O1	O2
Model player (Policy)	G1	**3.56**	8.33	7.82	10.22	10.96	8.83	11.54	10.01	10.02	7.75
	D1	7.1	**6.86**	6.46	7.96	7.63	7.35	9.51	7.28	7.82	7.22
	D2	6.71	8.05	**5**	7.25	7.77	8.03	10.04	8.01	8.19	8.75
	D3	4.63	7.85	5.63	7.19	7.74	8.13	8.69	7.34	7.24	6.8
	D4	14.17	16.05	10.98	13.82	**6.81**	12.15	13.18	12.74	12.08	10.84
	M1	4.24	8.04	5.94	7.08	7.67	**5.75**	8.48	6.4	7.07	5.82
	M2	5.61	8.69	6.75	7.4	7.26	7.14	**8.17**	6.16	7.46	7.27
	M3	4.98	7.54	5.79	**7.02**	7.22	6.27	**8.17**	**5.56**	6.58	**5.08**
	O1	5.73	8.69	7.23	8.14	7.65	6.76	8.31	6.39	**6.31**	6.33
	O2	4.63	8.22	7.92	8.99	8.62	8.75	9.9	8.06	8.74	5.6

split by four lines separated by 90°. Table 4 presents the confusion matrices for the movements after 2 s, 5 s, and 10 s. For all cases, the highest values are along the diagonal, and the method has stable F1-scores of 0.53, 0,52, and 0.53.

Cross-Evaluation. To investigate whether the policies have learned the behavior of the player it was trained on, policies trained on different players were cross-evaluated on each others' validation sequences. Table 5 shows the errors when using the model of one player to predict the movements of a different player. We note that the highest values are shown along the diagonal (or the players of the same player role). These results suggest that the best policies (in terms of global error) are achieved when using the policies for the specific player. We also noted that policies from players with similar roles often exhibit similar behavior. The latter observations show that the policies in fact do capture different player behaviors. This opens the door for interesting future work in which one player may be exchanged for another player, in a given situation. This is illustrated in Fig. 3. Here, we show the predicted (and actual) movement of an offensive player (Fig. 3(a)), as well as the predicted movement of a defensive player put into the same situation (Fig. 3(b)). In this situation the opposition shoots, and we note that the defensive player would run backwards much further towards the own goal.

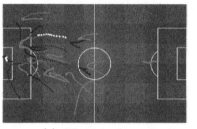   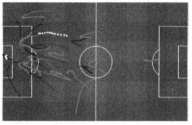

(a) Offensive player   (b) Defensive player

Fig. 3. Example rollouts of the same play with different policies.

6   Conclusion

In this paper we presented a method to predict player movement based on imitation learning, evaluated it using a large-scale 2019 dataset from the top-tier soccer league in Sweden (Allsvenskan). Our evaluation provides insights into how to best apply the method on movement traces in soccer. For example, we show that there is value in using relative actions, that a limited time window often is sufficient to achieve good accuracy, and that there is value in using data also from other players during the pre-training phase. We also validate the accuracy of the models (e.g., with regards to time and player role) and provide insights regarding how well different policies capture the relative behaviors of different player roles (e.g., similarities and differences between different player roles), gleaning some insights into how different player behaviors can be compared with the use of rollout using different player profiles. The latter highlight the value of these types of policies and open interesting directions for future work, including investigations on the effect of pre-training only on similar roles as the modelled player. Further, another direction for future research is multi-agent modelling. By cross-updating all player states between each time step the multi-agent approach would model the full dynamics and interactions of the players and not just a single player given a situation.

References

1. Andrienko, G., et al.: Visual analysis of pressure in football. Data Min. Knowl. Discov. **31**(6), 1793–1839 (2017). https://doi.org/10.1007/s10618-017-0513-2
2. Bialkowski, A., Lucey, P., Carr, P., Matthews, I.A., Sridharan, S., Fookes, C.: Discovering team structures in soccer from spatiotemporal data. IEEE Trans. Knowl. Data Eng. **28**(10), 2596–2605 (2016). https://doi.org/10.1109/TKDE.2016.2581158
3. Bialkowski, A., Lucey, P., Carr, P., Yue, Y., Sridharan, S., Matthews, I.: Large-scale analysis of soccer matches using spatiotemporal tracking data. In: Kumar, R., Toivonen, H., Pei, J., Huang, J.Z., Wu, X. (eds.) Proceedings of the 2014 IEEE International Conference on Data Mining, pp. 725–730 (2014)

4. Bojinov, I., Bornn, L.: The pressing game: optimal defensive disruption in soccer. In: 10th MIT Sloan Sports Analytics Conference (2016)
5. Brandt, M., Brefeld, U.: Graph-based approaches for analyzing team interaction on the example of soccer. In: Davis, J., van Haaren, J., Zimmermann, A. (eds.) Proceedings of the 2nd Workshop on Machine Learning and Data Mining for Sports Analytics. CEUR Workshop Proceedings, vol. 1970, pp. 10–17 (2015)
6. Bransen, L., Robberechts, P., Haaren, J.V., Davis, J.: Choke or shine? Quantifying soccer players' abilities to perform under mental pressure. In: 13th MIT Sloan Sports Analytics Conference (2019)
7. Cintia, P., Rinzivillo, S., Pappalardo, L.: Network-based measures for predicting the outcomes of football games. In: Davis, J., van Haaren, J., Zimmermann, A. (eds.) Proceedings of the 2nd Workshop on Machine Learning and Data Mining for Sports Analytics. CEUR Workshop Proceedings, vol. 1970, pp. 46–54 (2015)
8. Decroos, T., Dzyuba, V., Van Haaren, J., Davis, J.: Predicting soccer highlights from spatio-temporal match event streams. In: Proceedings of the 31st AAAI Conference on Artificial Intelligence, pp. 1302–1308 (2017)
9. Decroos, T., Van Haaren, J., Dzyuba, V., Davis, J.: STARSS: a spatio-temporal action rating system for soccer. In: Davis, J., Kaytoue, M., Zimmermann, A. (eds.) Proceedings of the 4th Workshop on Machine Learning and Data Mining for Sports Analytics. CEUR Workshop Proceedings, vol. 1971, pp. 11–20 (2017)
10. Eggels, H., van Elk, R., Pechenizkiy, M.: Explaining soccer match outcomes with goal scoring opportunities predictive analytics. In: van Haaren, J., Kaytoue, M., Davis, J. (eds.) Proceedings of the 3rd Workshop on Machine Learning and Data Mining for Sports Analytics. CEUR Workshop Proceedings, vol. 1842 (2016)
11. Fernandez, J., Bornn, L., Cervone, D.: Decomposing the immeasurable sport: a deep learning expected possession value framework for soccer. In: 13th MIT Sloan Sports Analytics Conference (2019)
12. Fernando, T., Wei, X., Fookes, C., Sridharan, S., Lucey, P.: Discovering methods of scoring in soccer using tracking data. In: Lucey, P., Yue, Y., Wiens, J., Morgan, S. (eds.) Proceedings of the 2nd KDD Workshop on Large Scale Sports Analytics (2015)
13. Gudmundsson, J., Wolle, T.: Football analysis using spatio-temporal tools. Comput. Environ. Urban Syst. **47**, 16–27 (2014). https://doi.org/10.1016/j.compenvurbsys.2013.09.004
14. Gyarmati, L., Anguera, X.: Automatic extraction of the passing strategies of soccer teams. In: Lucey, P., Yue, Y., Wiens, J., Morgan, S. (eds.) Proceedings of the 2nd KDD Workshop on Large Scale Sports Analytics (2015)
15. Gyarmati, L., Stanojevic, R.: QPass: a merit-based evaluation of soccer passes. In: Lucey, P., Yue, Y., Wiens, J., Morgan, S. (eds.) Proceedings of the 3rd KDD Workshop on Large Scale Sports Analytics (2016)
16. Van Haaren, J., Davis, J., Hannosset, S.: Strategy discovery in professional soccer match data. In: Lucey, P., Yue, Y., Wiens, J., Morgan, S. (eds.) Proceedings of the 3rd KDD Workshop on Large Scale Sports Analytics (2016)
17. Van Haaren, J., Dzyuba, V., Hannosset, S., Davis, J.: Automatically discovering offensive patterns in soccer match data. In: Fromont, E., De Bie, T., van Leeuwen, M. (eds.) IDA 2015. LNCS, vol. 9385, pp. 286–297. Springer, Cham (2015). https://doi.org/10.1007/978-3-319-24465-5_25
18. He, M., Cachucho, R., Knobbe, A.: Football player's performance and market value. In: Davis, J., van Haaren, J., Zimmermann, A. (eds.) Proceedings of the 2nd Workshop on Machine Learning and Data Mining for Sports Analytics. CEUR Workshop Proceedings, vol. 1970, pp. 87–95 (2015)

19. Ho, J., Ermon, S.: Generative adversarial imitation learning. In: Lee, D.D., Sugiyama, M., Luxburg, U.V., Guyon, I., Garnett, R. (eds.) Advances in Neural Information Processing Systems, vol. 29, pp. 4565–4573 (2016). http://papers.nips.cc/paper/6391-generative-adversarial-imitation-learning.pdf

20. Hochreiter, S., Schmidhuber, J.: Long short-term memory. Neural Comput. **9**(8), 1735–1780 (1997). https://doi.org/10.1162/neco.1997.9.8.1735

21. Horton, M., Gudmundsson, J., Chawla, S., Estephan, J.: Classification of passes in football matches using spatiotemporal data. In: Lucey, P., Yue, Y., Wiens, J., Morgan, S. (eds.) Proceedings of the 1st KDD Workshop on Large Scale Sports Analytics (2014)

22. Jordet, G., Bloomfield, J., Heijmerikx, J.: The hidden foundation of field vision in English Premier League (EPL) soccer players. In: 7th MIT Sloan Sports Analytics Conference (2013)

23. Kim, K., Grundmann, M., Shamir, A., Matthews, I.A., Hodgins, J.K., Essa, I.A.: Motion fields to predict play evolution in dynamic sport scenes. In: The Twenty-Third IEEE Conference on Computer Vision and Pattern Recognition, CVPR 2010, San Francisco, CA, USA, 13–18 June 2010, pp. 840–847 (2010). https://doi.org/10.1109/CVPR.2010.5540128

24. Lasek, J.: EURO 2016 predictions using team rating systems. In: van Haaren, J., Kaytoue, M., Davis, J. (eds.) Proceedings of the 3rd Workshop on Machine Learning and Data Mining for Sports Analytics. CEUR Workshop Proceedings, vol. 1842 (2016)

25. Le, H., Kang, A., Yue, Y., Carr, P.: Smooth imitation learning for online sequence prediction. In: Balcan, M.F., Weinberger, K.Q. (eds.) Proceedings of The 33rd International Conference on Machine Learning. Proceedings of Machine Learning Research, vol. 48, pp. 680–688 (2016). http://proceedings.mlr.press/v48/le16.html

26. Le, H.M., Carr, P., Yue, Y., Lucey, P.: Data-driven ghosting using deep imitation learning. In: 11th MIT Sloan Sports Analytics Conference (2017)

27. Le, H.M., Yue, Y., Carr, P., Lucey, P.: Coordinated multi-agent imitation learning. In: Precup, D., Teh, Y.W. (eds.) Proceedings of the 34th International Conference on Machine Learning, ICML 2017, Sydney, NSW, Australia, 6–11 August 2017, pp. 1995–2003 (2017). http://proceedings.mlr.press/v70/le17a.html

28. Lucey, P., Bialkowski, A., Carr, P., Foote, E., Matthews, I.: Characterizing multi-agent team behavior from partial team tracings: evidence from the English Premier League. In: Hoffmann, J., Selman, B. (eds.) 26th AAAI Conference on Artificial Intelligence, pp. 1387–1393 (2012)

29. Lucey, P., Bialkowski, A., Monfort, M., Carr, P., Matthews, I.: "Quality vs quantity": improved shot prediction in soccer using strategic features from spatiotemporal data. In: 9th MIT Sloan Sports Analytics Conference (2015)

30. Maystre, L., Kristof, V., Ferrer, A.J.G., Grossglauser, M.: The player kernel: learning team strengths based on implicit player contributions. In: van Haaren, J., Kaytoue, M., Davis, J. (eds.) Proceedings of the 3rd Workshop on Machine Learning and Data Mining for Sports Analytics. CEUR Workshop Proceedings, vol. 1842 (2016)

31. Nsolo, E., Lambrix, P., Carlsson, N.: Player valuation in european football. In: Brefeld, U., Davis, J., Van Haaren, J., Zimmermann, A. (eds.) MLSA 2018. LNCS (LNAI), vol. 11330, pp. 42–54. Springer, Cham (2019). https://doi.org/10.1007/978-3-030-17274-9_4

32. Osa, T., Pajarinen, J., Neumann, G., Bagnell, J.A., Abbeel, P., Peters, J.: An algorithmic perspective on imitation learning (2018)

33. Ross, S., Gordon, G., Bagnell, D.: A reduction of imitation learning and structured prediction to no-regret online learning. In: Gordon, G., Dunson, D., Dudík, M. (eds.) Proceedings of the Fourteenth International Conference on Artificial Intelligence and Statistics. Proceedings of Machine Learning Research, vol. 15, pp. 627–635 (2011). http://proceedings.mlr.press/v15/ross11a.html

34. Salustowicz, R., Wiering, M., Schmidhuber, J.: Learning team strategies: soccer case studies. Mach. Learn. **33**(2–3), 263–282 (1998). https://doi.org/10.1023/A: 1007570708568

35. Sammut, C.: Behavioral cloning. In: Sammut, C., Webb, G.I. (eds.) Encyclopedia of Machine Learning, pp. 93–97. Springer, Boston (2010). https://doi.org/10.1007/ 978-0-387-30164-8_69

36. Sarkar, S., Chakraborty, S.: Pitch actions that distinguish high scoring teams: findings from five European football leagues in 2015–16. J. Sports Anal. **4**(1), 1–14 (2018). https://doi.org/10.3233/JSA-16161

37. Schultze, S.R., Wellbrock, C.M.: A weighted plus/minus metric for individual soccer player performance. J. Sports Anal. **4**(2), 121–131 (2018). https://doi.org/10. 3233/JSA-170225

38. Sha, L., et al.: Interactive sports analytics: an intelligent interface for utilizing trajectories for interactive sports play retrieval and analytics. ACM Trans. Comput.-Hum. Interact. **25**(2), 13:1–13:32 (2018). https://doi.org/10.1145/3185596

39. Vercruyssen, V., Raedt, L.D., Davis, J.: Qualitative spatial reasoning for soccer pass prediction. In: van Haaren, J., Kaytoue, M., Davis, J. (eds.) Proceedings of the 3rd Workshop on Machine Learning and Data Mining for Sports Analytics. CEUR Workshop Proceedings, vol. 1842 (2016)

40. Vroonen, R., Decroos, T., Haaren, J.V., Davis, J.: Predicting the potential of professional soccer players. In: Davis, J., Kaytoue, M., Zimmermann, A. (eds.) Proceedings of the 4th Workshop on Machine Learning and Data Mining for Sports Analytics. CEUR Workshop Proceedings, vol. 1971, pp. 1–10 (2017)

41. Yam, D.: A data driven goalkeeper evaluation framework. In: 13th MIT Sloan Sports Analytics Conference (2019)

Other Team Sports

Stats Aren't Everything: Learning Strengths and Weaknesses of Cricket Players

Swarup Ranjan Behera[✉] and Vijaya V. Saradhi

Indian Institute of Technology Guwahati, Guwahati, Assam, India
{b.swarup,saradhi}@iitg.ac.in

Abstract. Strengths and weaknesses of individual players are understood informally by players themselves, coaches, and team management. However, there is no specific computational method to obtain strengths and weaknesses. The objective of this work is to obtain rules describing the strengths and weaknesses of cricket players. Instead of looking at the traditional statistics, which are nothing but the raw counts of certain events in the game, we focus on cricket text commentaries, which are written narratives giving a detailed description of a minute-by-minute account of the game while it is unfolding.

Keywords: Text mining · Cricket analytics · Dimentionality reduction

1 Introduction

Cricket is a sport played by tens of thousands and loved by billions of people from all corners of the globe [1]. Cricket is known for recording every detail. A huge amount of data in the form of scorecards, video broadcasts, commentary, and coverage articles is generated in every match. Statistics have been employed widely for years on the generated data. While interesting, the focus of the analysis has primarily been at an aggregate level. Cricket text commentary, on the contrary, is a rich source of fine-grained details about each delivery of the game.

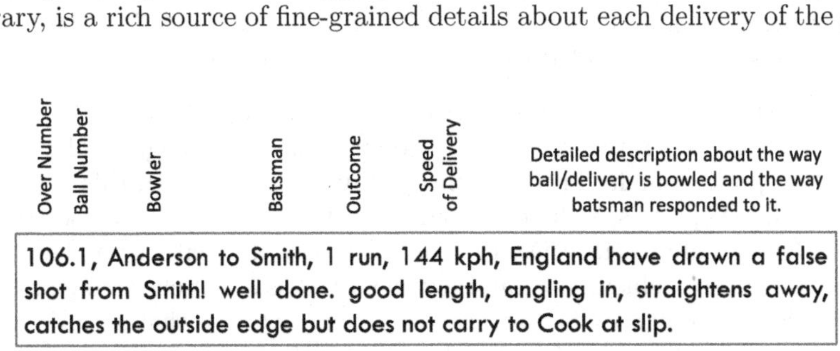

Over Number	Ball Number	Bowler	Batsman	Outcome	Speed of Delivery	Detailed description about the way ball/delivery is bowled and the way batsman responded to it.

106.1, Anderson to Smith, 1 run, 144 kph, England have drawn a false shot from Smith! well done. good length, angling in, straightens away, catches the outside edge but does not carry to Cook at slip.

Fig. 1. Example of cricket text commentary.

U. Brefeld et al. (Eds.): MLSA 2020, CCIS 1324, pp. 79–88, 2020.
https://doi.org/10.1007/978-3-030-64912-8_7

Consider an example of cricket text commentary presented in Fig. 1. This commentary describes the first delivery in the 107th over of the game. Bowler Anderson has bowled this delivery to the batsman Smith. The outcome of the ball is one run. The speed of the delivery is 144 kph (kilometer per hour). The rest of the text is unstructured and describes how the ball is delivered and how the batsman played it. For instance, this commentary describes several bowling features, such as length (*good length*) and movement (*angling in*). Similarly, it describes batting features such as response (*outside edge*) pointing to the batsman's imperfection. The words *false shot* emphasizes the imperfection and points to batsman's weakness against good length and angling in delivery. If we consistently observe poor performance by the batsman on similar deliveries, we can conclude that playing such deliveries is batsman's weakness. Such detailed weakness rules are far more expressive and useful than simple statistics such as batting average and strike rate.

The central idea of this work is to show the usefulness of cricket text commentary data in mining the strength and weakness rules of cricket players. To this end, we discuss two of our recently published works [2,3]. There are three tasks involved in learning the strength and weakness rules:

– *Text Commentary Collection.* We have collected a large and first-of-its-kind dataset of over one million deliveries, covering all international cricket Test matches in the last thirteen years (Sect. 2).
– *Feature Extraction.* We propose specific methods for data preprocessing and information extraction from text commentary. We propose several domain-specific features to represent each delivery with fine-grained details. This is the first work that proposes such a detailed representation of deliveries (Sect. 3).
– *Rule Learning* (Sect. 4).
  • For the first work [2], we use correspondence analysis [4,5] for dimensionality reduction, biplots [6] to visualize the data in two dimensions, and derive the strength and weakness rules using cosine similarity. The data, code, and results are provided in https://bit.ly/2SwCQ5r.
  • For the second work [3], we have mined the temporal changes in the obtained strength and weakness rules using three-way correspondence analysis [7], which internally uses tucker tensor decomposition [8]. The extracted temporal changes are plotted in a line plot. The data, code, and results are provided in https://bit.ly/2OL0Ujh.

The novelty of our work is two-fold: input data and output results. To the best of our knowledge, this is the first attempt to mine players' strength and weakness rules in the sports domain. From the perspective of text mining, this is the first attempt to mine sports-specific text commentary. Strengths and weaknesses do not have definite and distinct classes. Therefore they can neither be viewed as a text categorization problem, nor can they be viewed as a text clustering problem. A differentiating factor specific to cricket commentary text is that majority of the technical words used in the cricketing domain are *stop words* in the conventional text mining literature. Thus, this particular application of mining cricket text commentary is an important one from the text modeling context.

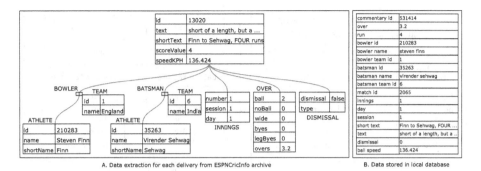

A. Data extraction for each delivery from ESPNCricInfo archive   B. Data stored in local database

Fig. 2. Collection of cricket text commentaries from ESPNCricInfo archive.

2 Text Commentary Collection

Cricket has multiple formats of the game, of which the *Test cricket* format is considered for the present work. EspnCricInfo[1] is selected as the data source. This is a sports news website exclusively dedicated to the game of cricket. It provides the most comprehensive repository of cricket text commentary. The earliest documented text commentary available for the Test matches dates back to 2006. To collect text commentary associated with a given Test match, one must first obtain the season and series of which this particular match is a part. In addition, match and innings IDs and associated URLs need to be formulated from ESPN-CricInfo's archive. This information is used to acquire the text commentaries for a given match. This procedure is repeated for all the matches played between May 2006 to April 2019. Total text commentaries of 1,088,570 deliveries are collected spanning thirteen years. The collected deliveries account for a total of 550 international Test cricket matches. Figure 2 demonstrates, with an example, the information extracted for each text commentary. The text commentaries are stored in a local database.

3 Feature Extraction

Each text commentary can be divided into two parts: structured and unstructured. Refer Fig. 3(A) to understand the structure of text commentary data. The structured part (red-colored text) is located at the beginning of each commentary. It describes the exact over number, delivery number, name of the bowler, name of the batsman, and delivery outcome. After this, the unstructured text commentary (blue-colored text) will optionally describe various bowling features (line, length, and speed of the delivery, etc.), batting features (batsman's response, footwork, and shot selection, etc.), and subjective opinion of the commentator about how the batsman performed.

---

[1] http://www.espncricinfo.com/.

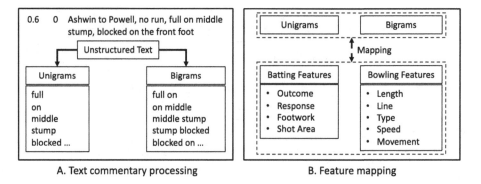

A. Text commentary processing   B. Feature mapping

Fig. 3. Text commentary processing and feature extraction. (Color figure online)

The extraction of information from the structured part is a straightforward task. However, information extraction from the unstructured part requires non-trivial efforts. Domain-specific technical vocabulary is dominantly observed in the unstructured part of text commentary. However, this technical vocabulary has fundamental challenges - (i) Each document (commentary for a particular delivery) comprises of a few tens of words. Due to this sparsity, we cannot apply term frequency based models. (ii) Each document contains technical words that fall into the category of stop words in other application domains. A non-exhaustive list is - *off, on, up, across, behind, back, out, into, away*. Unlike other text datasets, we cannot directly apply stop word removal to our dataset. (iii) Technical words alone (unigram) are not sufficient as the same word can have a different meaning in a commentary depending on the context of use (for batsman or bowler). Thus, the traditional off the shelf text representation models are not suitable due to the sparsity and the high technicality of the data.

To overcome these three challenges, domain-specific batting features and bowling features are identified. Each feature is represented as a set of unigrams and bigrams such that the identified set corresponds to the feature in question

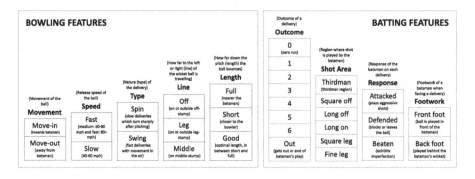

Fig. 4. Batting features and bowling features.

and is represented as feature definition. For example, the corresponding uni-grams and bigrams for the batting feature *beaten* are: miss, beat, poor shot, defeat, edge, miss hit, inside edge, and knock down. The exhaustive list of bat-ting and bowling features is provided in Fig. 4. This feature definition is obtained by consulting the cricket experts (institute level cricket players and coaches). A total of 19 batting features and 12 bowling features are identified.

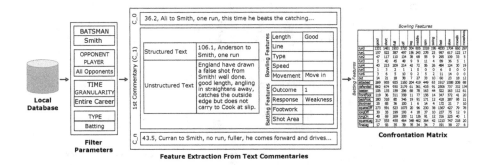

Fig. 5. Feature representation in the form of confrontation matrix.

Feature Representation. A confrontation matrix is constructed for each player using the batting and bowling features extracted from deliveries in which he/she is a part. In a confrontation matrix, rows stand for batting features, and columns represent bowling features. Each entry in this matrix represents the count of co-occurrence of respective feature values. For player-specific analysis, one has to first obtain a subset of text commentary. The extraction of this subset depends on a filter tuple having four elements $\langle player, opponentplayer, time, type \rangle$, where (a) the first two elements can be a single-player or a group of players, (b) *time* can be per session, per day, per innings, per match, per series, or an entire career, and (c) *type* can be batting or bowling, depending on whether we want to analyze the batting or bowling of the player in focus. Figure 5 shows the confrontation matrix construction for batsman Steve Smith. This matrix is constructed using only the deliveries where Steve Smith is involved as the batsman. This matrix is of size 19×12 in which rows correspond to batting features of the player, and columns correspond to bowling features of opponent players. Every element in this matrix corresponds to how the batsman is confronted with the bowlers. For example, how many numbers of times batsman has shown aggression on short length deliveries? The first entry in this matrix is 1331, which accounts for the number of times Steve Smith has scored 0 runs against the good length balls in his entire career against all opponent bowlers.

4   Rule Learning

In this section, a computational approach for strength and weakness rule construction of every individual player is first presented, followed by the temporal changes of strength and weakness rules for each player.

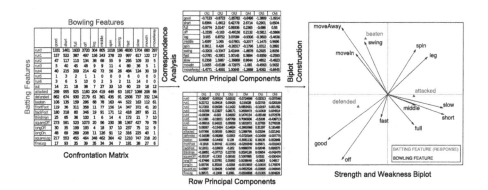

Fig. 6. Mining strength and weakness rules of batsman Steve Smith using correspondence analysis.

4.1   Learning Strength and Weakness Rules of Cricket Players

Both the bowling features and batting features in the confrontation matrix are in a high dimensional space. Dimensionality reduction methods are traditionally employed for reducing the number of variables and capturing the discriminative variables. In the present context, batting features (row variables) and bowling features (column variables) are discrete random variables. So, we use Correspondence Analysis (CA) [4,5], a multivariate statistical technique, to obtain a low-dimensional subspace that contains the batting (row) features and bowling (column) features. The central idea in CA is to test the independence of events, namely row variables, and column variables. If two events are not independent, then the equality does not hold; this points to the relationship between row variables and column variables. This relationship is captured in CA. Refer to Fig. 6 for the steps involved in learning the strength and weakness rules. Applying CA on the confrontation matrix, we obtain the row principal components and column principal components and plot them on a two-dimensional biplot [6]. The row (batting) and column (bowling) vectors with the highest inner product values are the closest vectors and positively correlated in the biplot. These two vectors constitute a strength rule when the selected batting feature is *attacked* or a weakness rule when the selected batting feature is *beaten*.

Figure 7 is the biplot for batsman Steve Smith representing only his response (for clarity) on various deliveries. In this biplot, the top three bowling vectors close to batting vector *attacked* are *slow, short* and *middle*. Thus the inferred strength rule is *"Smith attacks deliveries that are slow or short-pitched or bowled on middle stump"*. Similarly, the top three bowling vectors close to batting vector *beaten* are *swing, move away* and *move in*. Thus the inferred weakness rule is *"Smith gets beaten on deliveries that are swinging, moving away or moving in"*. We encourage the readers to go through our paper [2] for the detailed rule mining process and validation of the obtained rules.

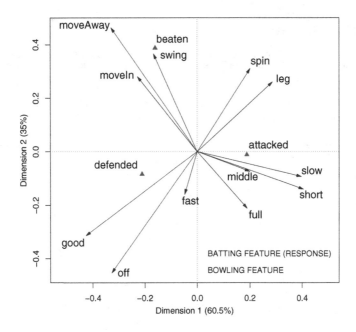

Fig. 7. Smith's response biplot.

4.2 Temporal Changes in Strength and Weakness Rules of Cricket Players

The objective is to graphically display the associations between the three variables: batting features, bowling features, and time (in years). That is, year-wise changes in strength and weakness rules are obtained. To this end, year-wise confrontation matrices are constructed for each batsman and bowler. Year-wise confrontation matrices for a player will result in a three-dimensional confrontation tensor. The analysis of the association between the variables of a three-dimensional tensor requires a different approach than CA. In order to retain the time association with batting or bowling features, the temporal changes in strength and weakness rules are computed through the Three-Way Correspondence Analysis (TWCA) [4] and are visualized through the factors in TWCA

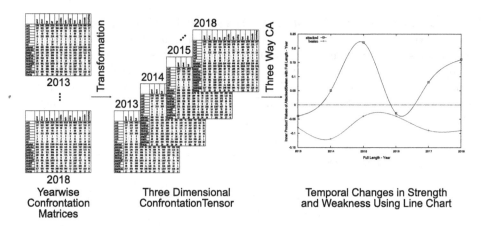

Fig. 8. Mining temporal changes in strength and weakness of batsman Steve Smith using three way correspondence analysis.

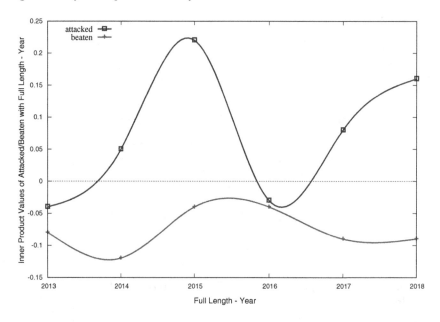

Fig. 9. Smith's strength and weakness on full-length deliveries over the years. (Color figure online)

(Refer to Fig. 8). The inner product of the principal components (batting and bowling-time) enables us to reconstruct the original three-way confrontation tensor and allows for a numerical assessment of the three-way association. A higher value of the inner product between a batting feature and a coded bowling-time feature indicates a high strength of association, while a lower value of inner product indicates a relatively low strength of association. To visualize the year wise changes, we plot the inner product values in a line plot. Figure 9 shows batsman Steve Smith's change in the strength rule (blue-colored line) namely *attack* strategy on *full length* deliveries. He has shown an increase in attacking full-length deliveries between the years 2013 and 2015 (both inclusive). However, in the 2016 year, he struggled with full-length deliveries. He once again showed strength in the full-length deliveries in 2017 and subsequent years. A similar analysis can be performed on the weakness rule (red-colored line) of *beaten* on *full length* deliveries for this player. We encourage the readers to go through our paper [3] for the detailed temporal rule mining process.

5   Related Work

As this contribution is an application specific to the sports domain, to the best of authors' knowledge, identifying a player's strengths and weaknesses rules in the cricket domain is not attempted in the literature. The book by Albert et al. [1] provides a comprehensive list of statistical methods on various sporting domains. Schumaker et al. [9] list the data-mining efforts on various sports. Cricket analysis has been extensively studied in the past years. Specifically, many researchers have contributed to the tactical analysis of cricket data. Statistical methods, for task such as target-resetting [10], player-performance [11, 12], match-simulation [9, 13], and tactis [14, 15] were introduced to aid the analysis from various perspectives. When a match is interrupted due to bad weather, target re-setting plays a major role. Duckworth and Lewis [10] proposed a method (DL-method) for target re-setting, which is adopted by International Cricket Council (ICC). Iyer and Sharda [11] employed neural networks to predict the performance of cricket players based on the player's past performance. The correlation of winning a game to different batting combinations and the run rate was identified by [13]. Scarf and Akhtar [14] proposed in test cricket whether teams should declare at various stages of matches and under different circumstances. All of the above-discussed methods capture information on an aggregate level and fail to look at various fine-grained details.

6   Conclusion

Cricket analytics predominantly centers around the traditional statistics, which are nothing but the raw counts of certain events in the game. For the first time, the utility of the cricket text commentary data is demonstrated. The analysis is focused on the computation of strength and weakness rules and their temporal changes. In this work, correspondence analysis and three-way correspondence analysis are shown to be suitable methods for the computation of such tasks. The strength and weakness rules will help analysts, coaches, and team management to build game strategies.

References

1. Albert, J., Glickman, M.E., Swartz, T.B., Koning, R.H.: Handbook of Statistical Methods and Analyses in Sports. Chapman & Hall/CRC Handbooks of Modern Statistical Methods. CRC Press, Taylor & Francis, Boca Raton (2016)
2. Behera, S.R., Agrawal, P., Awekar, A., Vedula, V.S.: Mining strengths and weaknesses of cricket players using short text commentary. In: 18th IEEE International Conference On Machine Learning And Applications (ICMLA), Boca Raton, FL, USA, pp. 673–679 (2019). https://doi.org/10.1109/ICMLA.2019.00122
3. Behera, S.R., Vedula, V.S.: Mining temporal changes in strengths and weaknesses of cricket players using tensor decomposition. In: 28th European Symposium on Artificial Neural Networks, Computational Intelligence and Machine Learning (ESANN), Bruges, Belgium (2020)
4. Beh, E.J., Lombardo, R.: Correspondence Analysis: Theory, Practice and New Strategies. Wiley Series in Probability and Statistics. Wiley, Chichester (2014)
5. Greenacre, M.: Correspondence Analysis in Practice. Chapman & Hall/CRC Interdisciplinary Statistics Series. CRC Press, Taylor & Francis, Boca Raton (2017)
6. Gabriel, K.R.: The biplot graphic display of matrices with application to principal component analysis. Biometrika **58**(3), 453–467 (1971)
7. Carlier, A., Kroonenberg, P.M.: Decompositions and biplots in three-way correspondence analysis. Psychometrika **61**, 355–373 (1996). https://doi.org/10.1007/BF02294344
8. Tucker, L.R.: Some mathematical notes on three-mode factor analysis. Psychometrika **31**, 279–311 (1966). https://doi.org/10.1007/BF02289464
9. Schumaker, R.P., Solieman, O.K., Chen, H.: Sports Data Mining. Springer, Boston (2010). https://doi.org/10.1007/978-1-4419-6730-5
10. Duckworth, F.C., Lewis, A.J.: A fair method for resetting the target in interrupted one-day cricket matches. J. Oper. Res. Soc. **49**(3), 220–227 (1998)
11. Iyer, S.R., Sharda, R.: Prediction of athletes performance using neural networks: an application in cricket team selection. Expert Syst. Appl. **36**(3), 5510–5522 (2009)
12. Saikia, H., Bhattacharjee, D., Lemmer, H.H.: A double weighted tool to measure the fielding performance in cricket. Int. J. Sports Sci. Coach. **7**(4), 699–713 (2012)
13. Allsopp, P.E., Clarke, S.R.: Rating teams and analysing outcomes in one-day and test cricket. J. Roy. Stat. Soc. Ser. A **167**(4), 657–667 (2004)
14. Scarf, P., Akhtar, S.: An analysis of strategy in the first three innings in test cricket: declaration and the follow-on. J. Oper. Res. Soc. **62**(11), 1931–1940 (2011). https://doi.org/10.1057/jors.2010.169
15. Roddick, J.F., Rice, S.: What's interesting about cricket? On thresholds and anticipation in discovered rules. SIGKDD Explor. Newsl. **3**(1), 1–5 (2001)

Prediction of Tiers in the Ranking of Ice Hockey Players

Timmy Lehmus Persson, Haris Kozlica, Niklas Carlsson,
and Patrick Lambrix$^{(\boxtimes)}$

Linköping University, Linköping, Sweden
patrick.lambrix@liu.se

Abstract. Many teams in the NHL utilize data analysis and employ data analysts. An important question for these analysts is to identify attributes and skills that may help predict the success of individual players. This study uses detailed player statistics from four seasons, player rankings from EA's NHL video games, and six machine learning algorithms to find predictive models that can be used to identify and predict players' ranking tier (top 10%, 25% and 50%). We also compare and contrast which attributes and skills best predict a player's success, while accounting for differences in player positions (goalkeepers, defenders and forwards). When comparing the resulting models, the Bayesian classifiers performed best and had the best sensitivity. The tree-based models had the highest specificity, but had trouble classifying the top 10% tier players. In general, the models were best at classifying forwards, highlighting that many of the official metrics are focused on the offensive measures and that it is harder to use official performance metrics alone to differentiate between top tier players.

1   Introduction

The success of a sports team depends a lot on the individual players making up that team. However, not all positions on a team are the same. In ice hockey there are three main types of players: goalkeepers, defenders and forwards. While evaluating players it is therefore important to take into account these types.

In this paper, we compare and contrast which attributes and skills best predict the success of individual ice hockey players in different positions. First, using the method in [14] we investigate which performance features were important for the three main position types in the National Hockey League (NHL) for four different seasons. For the data processing, feature selection and analysis we used R 3.6.3 and packages dplyr 0.8.3, ggplot2 3.0.0, gridExtra 2.3 and caret 6.0 as well as Weka 3.8.4 [6]. Our work (including [14] for football) distinguishes itself from other work on player valuation or player performance, by working with tiers of players, i.e., the top 10%, 25% and 50% players in different positions (in contrast to individual ratings). An exact ranking of players may not always be available, and for several tasks, e.g., scouting, an exact ranking of players is

© Springer Nature Switzerland AG 2020
U. Brefeld et al. (Eds.): MLSA 2020, CCIS 1324, pp. 89–100, 2020.
https://doi.org/10.1007/978-3-030-64912-8_8

not necessary. In these cases using tiers is a useful approximation. Further, we deal with many skills.

Second, we evaluate different techniques for generating prediction models for players belonging to the different top tiers of players. We used Weka 3.8.4 for estimation of the models. We found that the two Bayesian classifiers performed best and that, in general, the models were best at classifying forwards.

The remainder of the paper is organized as follows. Section 2 presents related work. Section 3 discusses the data sets and the data preparation. Sections 4 and 5 present the feature selection and prediction methods, respectively, and show and discuss the corresponding results. Finally, the paper concludes in Sect. 6.

2 Related Work

In many sports work has started on measuring player performance. For the sake of brevity, we address the related work in ice hockey.

Many of the models for evaluating player performance in ice hockey define a particular stat or evaluation measure that assigns values based on particular types of actions in the game. For instance, the well-known goal measure, assist measure, and the more recent Fenwick and Corsi measures[1] attribute a value to goal-scoring actions, to passes that lead to goals and to different types of shots, respectively. To deal with some of the weaknesses of traditional measures new approaches have been proposed, including regression models replacing the $+/-$ measure (e.g., [3,12,13]). One main recognized weakness is the lack of influence of the context in which the actions are performed. This is the basis of the work on added goal value [15] that attributes value to goals, but the value of the goal is dependent on the situation in which it is scored.

Recent works often take several kinds of actions into account for defining a measure. For instance, in [4] principal component analysis was performed based on 18 traditional measures and a performance measure based on the four most important components was proposed. Further, many of these approaches also take some context into account. For instance, event impacts for different kinds of actions in [19] are based on the probability that the event leads to a goal (for or against) in the next 20 s. Several works model the dynamics of an ice hockey game using Markov games (e.g., [7,22]). In [9,16,20,21] action-value Q-functions are learned with respect to different targets. The proposed measure in [9] showed the highest correlation to 12 out of 14 traditional measures compared to measures such as $+/-$, goal-above-replacement, win-above-replacement and expected goals. In [17] the action-value Q-functions are used to define variants of these player impact measures. In [11] action-value Q-functions are used to define measures for pairs of players. Player rankings used for the NHL draft are presented in [10,18].

---

[1] See, e.g., https://en.wikipedia.org/wiki/Analytics_(ice_hockey).

Table 1. Attributes for field players and goalkeepers. Attributes in italics were removed during data preparation.

Position	Attributes
Field players	Player, Age, Team, POS (position), GP (games played), G (goals), A (assists), *PTS* (points), +/−, PIM (penalty minutes), PS (point shares), EVG (even strength goals), PPG (powerplay goals), SHG (shorthanded goals), GWG (game-winning goals), EVA (even strength assists), PPA (powerplay assists) , SHA (shorthanded assistss), S (shots on goal), *S%* (shots on goal percentage), TOI (time on ice), *TOI/60*, BLK (blocks), HIT (hits), FWON (face-offs won), FOL (face-offs lost), *FO%* (face-off percentage), CF (Corsi For), CA (Corsi Against), *CF%* (Corsi For percentage), CF%Rel (Corsi For percentage relative), FF (Fenwick For), FA (Fenwick Against), *FF%* (Fenwick For percentage), FF%Rel (Fenwick For percentage relative), oiSH% (on ice shooting percentage), oiSV% (on-ice save percentage) *PDO*, oZS% (offensive zone start percentage), dZS% (defensive zone start percentage), TOI(EV) (time on ice even strength), TK (takeaways), GV (giveaways), E+/− (expected +/−), SAtt. (shot attempts), Thru% (through percentage), SHFT (shift length), EVTOI (even strength time on ice), GF/60 (even strength Goals For per 60 min), GA/60 (even strength Goals Against per 60 min), PPTOI (powerplay time on ice), *PPCF%Rel* (powerplay Corsi For percentage relative), *PPGF/60* (powerplay goals for per 60 min), *PPGA/60* (powerplay goals against per 60 min), SHTOI (shorthanded time on ice), *SHCF%Rel* (shorthanded Corsi For percentage relative), *SHGF/60* (shorthanded Goals For per 60 min), *SHGA/60* (shorthanded Goals Against per 60 min)
Goalkeepers	Player, Age, Team, GP (games played), GS (game starts), W (wins), L (losses), OTL (overtime losses), GA (goals against), SA (shots against), *SV* (saves), *SV%* (save percentage), *GAA* (goals against average), SO (shutouts), GPS (goalkeeper point shares), MIN (minutes), QS (quality starts), *QS%* (quality starts percentage), RBS (really bad starts), *GA%* (goals against percentage), *GSAA* (goals saved above average), G (goals), A (assists), PTS (points), PIM (penalty minutes)

3   Data Collection and Preparation

3.1   Data Collection

The data regarding players was taken from Hockey Reference[2] for the seasons 2015/16 to 2018/19. Different attributes were gathered for goalkeepers and field players. The lists of attributes are given in Table 1. Descriptions of the attributes are given in the extended version of this paper [8].

---

[2] https://www.hockey-reference.com/.

The ranking used as a response variable was directly taken from Electronic Arts NHL games between 2016 and 2019 (NHL17, NHL18, NHL19 and NHL20). We use the player rating value that is supposed to be a summary of a player's individual attributes[3]. The range for this value is between 1 and 99.

3.2   Data Preparation

The data was then split using player position: goalkeepers, defenders, and forwards[4], resulting in 12 data sets (3 player positions × 4 seasons). As some of the players did not have a rating in the NHL games, data about these players was removed. Table 2 shows the number of retained players per position and the number of removed players.

For each of the data sets, attributes that were combinations of other attributes were removed. For field players these are G, A, PTS, S%, TOI/60, FO%, CF%, FF%, and PDO. For goalkeepers these are SV, SV%, GAA and QS%. Further, G was removed for goalkeepers as no goalkeeper scored those seasons. For other attributes data was missing and it was decided to impute the value 0 (Thru%, oiSH%, oiSV%, oZS%, dZS%) or remove the attribute (PPCF%Rel, SHCF%Rel, PPGF/60, PPGA/60, SHGF/60, SHGA/60, GA%, GSAA). All temporal attributes were rewritten into seconds. The value for Team was set to the team for which the player played the most games or in case of a tie to the team in which the player ended the season. Numerical data was normalized using the min-max-method to values between 0 and 1.

Table 2. Number of players per position with ratings. In parentheses we show the number of players without ratings that were removed from the data set.

Season	Forwards	Defenders	Goalkeepers
2015/16	582 (10)	297 (9)	91 (1)
2016/17	572 (17)	287 (12)	90 (5)
2017/18	555 (28)	297 (10)	93 (2)
2018/19	545 (35)	302 (24)	87 (8)

The rating was used to create the top 10%, 25% and 50% tiers. However, as several players had the same rating it was not always possible to take a tier without having players with the same rating in the tier and outside the tier. Therefore, we decided to use a cutoff such that the actual percentages are less than or equal to the desired percentage for the tier. Using this strategy the actual percentages for the top 10%, 25% and 50% tiers for the different position and

---

[3] https://www.ea.com/games/nhl/nhl-20/ratings.
[4] In the original data the forwards were categorized as left wing, right wing, center and wing.

seasons were between 6.5% and 9.3%, 19.5% and 25%, and 39.6% and 49.3%, respectively. The exact numbers for each data set are given in [8].

For each of the data sets resulting from the steps above, we made an 80%–20% split where the 80% is used in the feature selection (Sect. 4) and as training set in the prediction (Sect. 5) while the 20% is used as test set in the prediction.

4 Feature Selection

4.1 Filter Method

Filter methods for feature selection examine data using statistical methods to determine which attributes are relevant. They often use relatively simple calculations and are often relatively fast. We used correlation-based feature selection (CFS) which aims to identify sets of attributes that are highly correlated to the classification, but not correlated with each other [5]. Essentially, CFS computes the Pearson correlation coefficient where all attributes have been standardized and uses this as a measure of merit for the attribute subsets. Further, we used 10-fold cross validation. This results in different subsets for the different runs. We retained the attributes that appeared in at least two of these subsets.

4.2 Wrapper Method

Wrapper methods try to identify which subsets of attributes give the best results when used in a model by testing combinations of attributes. Wrapper methods employ a supervised learning method to compute the merit of each subset and are thus dependent on the chosen learning method.

We used the machine learning methods Logistic Regression (LR), Naïve Bayes (NB), Bayesian Network (BN) with $\alpha = 0.1$ and $u = 1$, Decision Tree (DT) with $C = 0.25$ and $M = 2$, k-Nearest Neighbor (KNN) with $k = 3$ and Random Forest (RF) with $I = 100$. For the Bayesian methods the attributes should be of nominal type and therefore the values of all numeric-type attributes were discretized by creating ten intervals with a width of 0.1 and ranging from 0 to 1 [2].

We used the Weka settings $\epsilon = 0.01$ and $k = 5$. This means that we started from the empty set and used best-first search with backtracking after five consecutive non-improving nodes in the search tree. As measure for merit we used AUC. Each algorithm was run over 10 folds and for each attribute and each algorithm the number of folds that contained the attribute was registered. Then for each attribute the mean over this number for the different algorithms was computed and if this mean was larger than 2 the attribute was retained.

4.3 Results and Discussion

Table 3 shows the number of attributes that were retained per position, tier and season for both the filter and wrapper methods. Table 4 shows the most common attributes per position for the filter and wrapper methods. The full list of attributes for each data set is given in [8].

Table 3. Number of retained attributes for the filter and wrapper methods, respectively. (filter/wrapper).

Season	Tier	Goalkeepers	Defenders	Forwards
2015/16	Top 10%	3/7	9/13	10/11
	Top 25%	2/5	17/8	12/13
	Top 50%	5/5	21/11	22/14
2016/17	Top 10%	5/5	11/11	16/14
	Top 25%	5/5	13/12	14/11
	Top 50%	9/6	17/13	23/9
2017/18	Top 10%	2/3	6/9	8/9
	Top 25%	7/7	11/8	13/8
	Top 50%	5/7	18/12	11/11
2018/19	Top 10%	4/6	15/10	11/11
	Top 25%	6/3	13/18	13/10
	Top 50%	9/6	18/11	20/11

Table 4. Most common attributes per position for filter and wrapper methods.

G-filter	D-filter	F-filter	G-wrapper	D-wrapper	F-wrapper
QS(11)	PS(12)	PS(12)	SO(9)	PS(9)	PS(11)
W(10)	TOI(EV)(12)	PPA(12)	W(9)	TOI(EV) (8)	PPA(10)
GPS(8)	PPA(12)	TOI(EV)(12)	QS(8)	PPA(7)	TOI(EV)(9)
GP(6)	EVA(9)	SHFT(11)	GPS(6)	oiSH%(7)	EVTOI(9)
SO(6)	S(9)	EVTOI, PPTOI(9)	SA, GS(5)	SHG, EVTOI, GA/60, PPTOI(7)	PPTOI(9)

For goalkeepers W and QS were common for several tiers in the same season for both methods, while GPS was also common for the filter method. QS was important for all tiers over all seasons for the filter method. For the wrapper method SO was important over all seasons for the 25% and 50% tiers. For defenders PS and PPA were important for all tiers and all seasons for the filter method, while TOI(EV) and S appeared often. For the wrapper method PPTOI and TOI(EV) appeared in all tears for several seasons. For the top 10% tier GA/60 was important for all seasons for the wrapper method, while PPA was important for the top 25% tier. For forwards PS and PPA were important for the filter and wrapper methods and TOI(EV) for the filter method. SHFT was an important attribute for the filter method for forwards, but not so much for defenders. In general, S is more common for top 50% tier players, while PPA is most common for top 25% tier players. Interestingly, PPA is selected more often than EVA. Further, in contrast to the wrapper method, for the filter method it is more common that attributes for a particular tier are selected in different seasons. Season 2017/18 was different in two senses. First, more attributes were selected for defenders and forwards than for the other seasons. Secondly, PPTOI and EVTOI were often selected in other seasons, but not in 2017/18.

We note that many of the selected attributes for field players are measures related to offense (e.g., related to assists, goals and shots) or neutral (e.g., related to time on ice), but the most often occurring measure (PS) relates to both offense and defense. For defenders, there are additionally measures related to goals against. This may reflect the kinds of stats that are collected for players.

In the data preparation step we removed attributes that are combinations of other attributes and these included much used metrics (e.g., goals and assists), which hockey professionals would want to use. Therefore, we investigated whether these metrics 'appeared' in the results, meaning that the attributes on which they depend were selected. For goalkeepers QS% (combination of QS and GS) appeared often, while SV and SV% (combinations of SA and GA) appeared in filter data sets. We also note that whenever GA occurred, also GA% can be computed. Regarding field players, A (combination of EVA, PPA and SHA) appeared sometimes, but the interesting combination of EVA and PPA (which does not take into account boxplay) occurred often. To a lesser extent the same happened for G (combination of EVG, PPG and SHG). S% (combination of EVG, PPG, SHG and S) did not occur, but combinations of EVG, PPG and S, or EVG and S did. Further, also CF% (combination of CA and CF), FF% (combination of FA and FF), FO% (combination of FOW and FOL) and PDO (combination of oiSH% amd oiSV%) appeared in some data sets. For more information about the exact numbers of occurrences, see [8].

5   Prediction

5.1   Methods

For each data set that was used in the feature selection step, we then created two new data sets, one where we used the attributes selected by the filter method and one with the attributes selected by the wrapper method. For the top 10% and top 25% tier data sets we used SMOTE [1] to overcome the class imbalance. This oversampling technique synthetically determines copies of the instances of the minority class to be added to the data set to match the quantity of instances of the majority class.

5.2   Results and Discussion

A detailed performance of all algorithms on all data sets is given in [8]. Figure 1 shows specificity, AUC, F1, sensitivity and accuracy for different seasons, positions, tiers, filter/wrapper and machine learning algorithms. The largest variation among the measures was for F1. Figure 2 shows F1 for different positions and tiers with respect to season, filter/wrapper and machine learning algorithm.

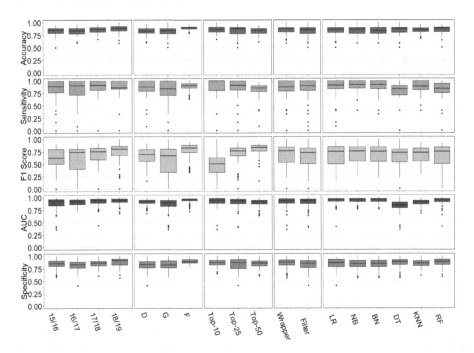

Fig. 1. Specificity, AUC, F1, sensitivity and accuracy for different seasons, positions, tiers, filter/wrapper and machine learning algorithms.

Overall, the choice between the filter and wrapper methods for different measures is not that important (Fig. 1), although for particular tiers and positions there may be a difference (e.g., goalkeepers top 10% and 25%, Fig. 2).

When comparing the resulting models, the two Bayesian classifiers were top performers for most data sets and evaluation measures and performed evenly across all combinations of comparisons. This is in line with the study in [14] regarding football. The tree-based models had the highest specificity, but had a lower sensitivity. They seemed to prioritize the majority class which resulted in lower performance when classifying the top 10% tier, and especially for the smaller data sets (e.g., goalkeepers). Overall, the models achieved high sensitivity, although for small data sets the tree-based models did not do well. In general, the models were best at classifying forwards, highlighting that many of the official metrics are focused on the offensive measures. This suggests that more work is needed to develop equally good defensive metrics. The models also achieved higher F1 for the top 50% highlighting that it is harder to differentiate between the highest rank top tier players using official performance metrics alone.

There is variation over the seasons, reflecting, among others, that different attributes were selected for different seasons.

A closer look at the misclassified players explains why the above problems are so hard. For example, of the top 10% forwards of the 2018/19 season, 19 players

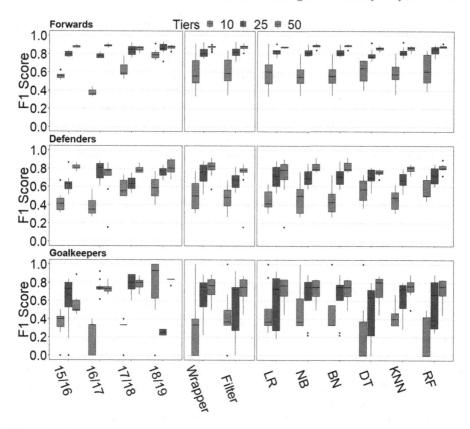

Fig. 2. F1 for different positions and tiers with respect to season, filter/wrapper and machine learning algorithm.

were misclassified by at least one out of 12 (2 × 6) combined models and the best model (BN) misclassified 8 players with the filter method and 10 with the wrapper method. However, some of these players either had weaker than normal years and therefore may have been classified lower than they normally would have by some models (e.g., Taylor Hall 4/12 wrong, Gabriel Landeskog 2/12 wrong, Joe Pavelski 1/12 wrong, and Auston Matthews 1/12 wrong, Patrice Bergeron 1/12 wrong), was a Rookie (Elias Pettersson 1/12 wrong) or were players outside the top 10% tier that were classified into this top tier at least once. For the first set we note that the most frequent player that should be in the set but sometimes is classified outside is Taylor Hall. He is a former Hart Trophy (league MVP) winner (2017/18 season) that had an injury plagued 2018/19 were he only played 33 out of 82 games. Similarly, the misclassification of the two most frequently misclassified players of the last set can also be explained. Teuvo Teravainen is an upcoming star who ranked 29th in the scoring race when the 2019/20 season shut down for a covid-19 break, and Evgenii Dadonov had a career year (scoring 72 points 2018/19) playing on a line with Aleksander Barkov and Jonathan

Huberdeau (which both finished with over 90 points). The lists of misclassified players for all data sets are given in [8].

A limitation of the study is that for the algorithms with many parameters, we did not perform experiments to find the optimal parameter setting, but usually used the default values. An area for future work is, therefore, to experiment with optimal settings as well as other algorithms. Further, there are some choices in the experiments that may have an influence on the results. For instance, the choice of the number of occurrences in the feature selection step influences which attributes to retain and thus the data sets on which the machine learning algorithms are evaluated. It would be interesting to investigate these choices in a systematic way. Another track for future work is to use player performance methods for ranking instead of the EA player rating and to compare the results of the different methods.

6   Conclusion

In this paper we used 6 different machine learning methods (Logistic regression, k-Nearest neighbour, Decision tree, Random forest, Naïve Bayes and Bayesian network) and 2 different feature selection methods (filter and wrapper) to predict players' ranking tier (top 10%, 25% and 50%) for 3 player positions (forwards, defenders, and goalkeepers), looking at 4 seasons (2015/16–2018/19). The study highlights key performance metrics for the different player categories and provides insights into the difference in the complexity of identifying the key attributes and skills that may help predict the success of individual players.

When comparing the resulting models, the two Bayesian classifiers performed best and had the best sensitivity. The tree-based models had the highest specificity, but had trouble classifying the top 10% tier players. In general, the models were best at classifying forwards, highlighting that many of the official metrics are focused on the offensive measures. The development of equally good defensive metrics still remains an open problem.

References

1. Chawla, N.V., Bowyer, K.W., Hall, L.O., Kegelmeyer, W.P.: SMOTE: synthetic minority over-sampling technique. J. Artif. Intell. Res. **16**, 321–357 (2002). https://doi.org/10.1613/jair.953
2. Dougherty, J., Kohavi, R., Sahami, M.: Supervised and unsupervised discretization of continuous features. In: Prieditis, A., Russell, S.J. (eds.) Machine Learning, Proceedings of the Twelfth International Conference on Machine Learning, pp. 194–202 (1995). https://doi.org/10.1016/b978-1-55860-377-6.50032-3
3. Gramacy, R.B., Jensen, S.T., Taddy, M.: Estimating player contribution in hockey with regularized logistic regression. J. Quant. Anal. Sports **9**, 97–111 (2013). https://doi.org/10.1515/jqas-2012-0001
4. Gu, W., Foster, K., Shang, J., Wei, L.: A game-predicting expert system using big data and machine learning. Expert Syst. Appl. **130**, 293–305 (2019). https://doi.org/10.1016/j.eswa.2019.04.025

5. Hall, M.: Correlation-based feature selection for machine learning. Ph.D. thesis, The University of Waikato, New Zealand (1999)
6. Hall, M., Frank, E., Holmes, G., Pfahringer, B., Reutemann, P., Witten, I.H.: The WEKA data mining software: an update. SIGKDD Explor. **11**(1), 10–18 (2009). https://doi.org/10.1145/1656274.1656278
7. Kaplan, E.H., Mongeon, K., Ryan, J.T.: A Markov model for hockey: manpower differential and win probability added. INFOR Inf. Syst. Oper. Res. **52**(2), 39–50 (2014). https://doi.org/10.3138/infor.52.2.39
8. Lehmus Persson, T., Kozlica, H., Carlsson, N., Lambrix, P.: Prediction of tiers in the ranking of ice hockey players - extended version (2020). https://www.ida.liu.se/~patla00/publications/mlsa2020-hockey-extended.pdf
9. Liu, G., Schulte, O.: Deep reinforcement learning in ice hockey for context-aware player evaluation. In: Lang, J. (ed.) Proceedings of the Twenty-Seventh International Joint Conference on Artificial Intelligence, pp. 3442–3448 (2018). https://doi.org/10.24963/ijcai.2018/478
10. Liu, Y., Schulte, O., Li, C.: Model trees for identifying exceptional players in the NHL and NBA drafts. In: Brefeld, U., Davis, J., Van Haaren, J., Zimmermann, A. (eds.) MLSA 2018. LNCS (LNAI), vol. 11330, pp. 93–105. Springer, Cham (2019). https://doi.org/10.1007/978-3-030-17274-9_8
11. Ljung, D., Carlsson, N., Lambrix, P.: Player pairs valuation in ice hockey. In: Brefeld, U., Davis, J., Van Haaren, J., Zimmermann, A. (eds.) MLSA 2018. LNCS (LNAI), vol. 11330, pp. 82–92. Springer, Cham (2019). https://doi.org/10.1007/978-3-030-17274-9_7
12. Macdonald, B.: A regression-based adjusted plus-minus statistic for NHL players. J. Quant. Anal. Sports **7**(3) (2011). https://doi.org/10.2202/1559-0410.1284
13. Macdonald, B.: An improved adjusted plus-minus statistic for nhl players. In: MIT Sloan Sports Analytics Conference (2011)
14. Nsolo, E., Lambrix, P., Carlsson, N.: Player valuation in European football. In: Brefeld, U., Davis, J., Van Haaren, J., Zimmermann, A. (eds.) MLSA 2018. LNCS (LNAI), vol. 11330, pp. 42–54. Springer, Cham (2019). https://doi.org/10.1007/978-3-030-17274-9_4
15. Pettigrew, S.: Assessing the offensive productivity of NHL players using in-game win probabilities. In: MIT Sloan Sports Analytics Conference (2015)
16. Routley, K., Schulte, O.: A Markov game model for valuing player actions in ice hockey. In: Meila, M., Heskes, T. (eds.) Uncertainty in Artificial Intelligence, pp. 782–791 (2015)
17. Sans Fuentes, C., Carlsson, N., Lambrix, P.: Player impact measures for scoring in ice hockey. In: Karlis, D., Ntzoufras, I., Drikos, S. (eds.) MathSport International 2019 Conference, pp. 307–317 (2019)
18. Schuckers, M.: Draft by numbers: using data and analytics to improve National Hockey League (NHL) player selection. In: MIT Sloan Sports Analytics Conference (2016)
19. Schuckers, M., Curro, J.: Total Hockey Rating (THoR): a comprehensive statistical rating of National Hockey League forwards and defensemen based upon all on-ice events. In: MIT Sloan Sports Analytics Conference (2013)
20. Schulte, O., Khademi, M., Gholami, S., Zhao, Z., Javan, M., Desaulniers, P.: A Markov Game model for valuing actions, locations, and team performance in ice hockey. Data Min. Knowl. Discov. **31**(6), 1735–1757 (2017). https://doi.org/10.1007/s10618-017-0496-z

21. Schulte, O., Zhao, Z., Javan, M., Desaulniers, P.: Apples-to-apples: clustering and ranking NHL players using location information and scoring impact. In: MIT Sloan Sports Analytics Conference (2017)
22. Thomas, A., Ventura, S.L., Jensen, S., Ma, S.: Competing process hazard function models for player ratings in ice hockey. Ann. Appl. Stat. **7**(3), 1497–1524 (2013). https://doi.org/10.1214/13-AOAS646

Individual Sports

A Machine Learning Approach for Road Cycling Race Performance Prediction

Leonid Kholkine[1]([✉]), Tom De Schepper[1], Tim Verdonck[2], and Steven Latré[1]

[1] Department of Computer Science, University of Antwerp - imec, Antwerp, Belgium
Leonid.Kholkine@uantwerpen.be
[2] Department of Mathematics, University of Antwerp, Antwerp, Belgium

Abstract. Predicting cycling race results has always been a task left to experts with a lot of domain knowledge. This is largely due to the fact that the outcomes of cycling races can be rather surprising and depend on an extensive set of parameters. Examples of such factors are, among others, the preparedness of a rider, the weather, the team strategy, and mechanical failure. However, we believe that due to the availability of historical data (e.g., race results, GPX files, and weather data) and the recent advances in machine learning, the prediction of the outcomes of cycling races becomes feasible. In this paper, we present a framework for predicting future race outcomes by using machine learning. We investigate the use of past performance race data as a good predictor. In particular, we focus on the Tour of Flanders as our proof-of-concept. We show, among others, that it is possible to predict the outcomes of a one-day race with similar or better accuracy than a human.

Keywords: Cycling race performance · Race result prediction · Road cycling · Machine learning

1 Introduction

The last decade, the interests in, and the possibilities of, sports analytics has known a drastic surge. This is largely due to the increased availability of training and competition data, often captured by wearables, across nearly all sports [7]. The captured data and corresponding insights can, for instance, be used to enhance training schemes, performance, and live sports broadcasting. The latter is, among others, the case in the broadcasting of road cycling races, where occasionally the power values (in Watts) of riders are reported. Based on the data it becomes also interesting to predict the chances of an athlete or team to win a certain race or game.

However, in the area of road cycling, the prediction of race performance is a very hard task. The main reason for this is that the outcome of a race, or the performance of a specific rider, depends on a large set of factors. For instance, the type of race, the road conditions, the team strategy, the current preparation and condition (both physically and mentally) of the rider, weather conditions,

© Springer Nature Switzerland AG 2020
U. Brefeld et al. (Eds.): MLSA 2020, CCIS 1324, pp. 103–112, 2020.
https://doi.org/10.1007/978-3-030-64912-8_9

mechanical errors, and the unpredictability of the race itself. As illustrated by Fig. 1, a review published by Atkinson et al. shows how a number of these factors are connected [4].

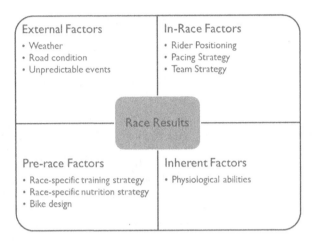

Fig. 1. Diagram showing the factors that influence cycling race results, adapted from [4]

Traditionally, to approach this problem, a lot of expert knowledge (often subjectively defined) is necessary to find the right patterns for predicting the performance. As the amount of available structured data that is produced is increasing ever so more (such as race results, power values, heart rate, weather, etc. . .), there is an opportunity to make this prediction more data-driven. Furthermore, Machine Learning (ML) algorithms have been successful in finding complex patterns in many different fields. Hence, in this paper, we propose a framework based on a ML algorithm to predict the outcomes for road cycling races.

Our contributions are threefold. First, we present a framework that can generate a prediction based on the past data of previous performance in races and the overall team performance. Second, we present a proof-of-concept that has been evaluated with the previous editions of the Tour of Flanders. Third, an in-depth evaluation of different features, and their importance, is conducted. The remainder of this paper is structured as follows. We start by presenting related work in Sect. 2. Section 3 gives an overview of the presented framework, while we present our case study in Sect. 4. We follow up with the results and discussion in Sect. 5 and, finally, conclude in Sect. 6.

2   Related Work

A variety of work has been done on predicting sports results using ML techniques and including team sports such as soccer or basketball. In [2] the authors used decision tree based ML to predict the outcomes of the Premier League matches. They also concluded that these methodologies have a better accuracy then Support Vector Machine (SVM). The authors of [14] analyzed on the importance of the features when predicting the outcome of NBA games. They found that doing a proper feature selection can increase the accuracy in around 2–4%. Furthermore, a study on how much luck and skill is involved in professional team sports was evaluated in [3]. The authors demonstrated that basketball is the sport that involves less luck in comparison with volleyball, soccer and handball. They have also demonstrated that when removing, on average, 20% of the teams from soccer, it becomes a random tournament. Even though no such study has been conducted on road cycling, it shows that there is a factor of luck involved in some sports.

While a lot research focuses on sports like soccer or basketball, also some work in the domain of (road) cycling exists which is described below. The authors of [11], a review of road cycling performance metrics, argue that there is a need for new methods which can quantify the effects of training loads and their implications for performance. The authors looked at different methodologies (e.g., mean power output metrics and binning methodologies), but none of them was perfect. The authors also considered a Neural Network (NN) approach, highlighting the potential due to the non-linear nature, but emphasized the need for large amounts of data. Additionally, a second concern is the poor explainability of the NN approach, as it is harder to explicitly identify causal relationships. Furthermore, Linear Regression (LR) and a NN architecture have been used to predict the time that it takes to complete a certain segment by "casual bikers" (non-professional bikers) [12]. The input features used are heart rate, attempt count, air temperature, humidity and wind (with direction and strength), while the output is a single value indicating the amount of time needed to complete the segment. The baseline is the mean of all segments for the single rider. The models did outperform the baseline, though due to low amount of data, both LR and a NN models proved to have a similar performance.

Moreover, in road cycling, two metrics that are very important in analysing the performance of the rider are the heart rate and the power output. In [8], the authors showed promising results in using a Long short-term memory (LSTM) model to predict the heart rate, trained with 15 male riders. The authors also speculate that the generated feature embedding can be used to cluster and classify similar training sessions. Note that even though promising results are showed, only laboratory values were used. In contrast, the authors of [9] created a model to predict real-time power output prediction during the Tour of France using only GPS and wind information. Using a mix of hand-crafted and automatic features, generated by a deep learning model, they managed to train a ML model capable of predicting the power output in real-time with an Mean Absolute Error (MAE) that is reduced by 56.79% compared to the physical model.

2.1 Predicting Cycling Performance in Race

Existing work that aims to predict the performance in actual races is rather limited. The work of [1] tries to predict the first Mean Maximum Power for various time periods for a certain race based on practice data. This work is done under specific training session conditions (in this case high altitude training) and only tries to predict the values for mountain stages. This is due to the fact that in these stages the output values depend mostly on individual rider performance. Even though the results look promising, the proposed models are trained on 41 races and 23 training sessions for only 3 professional riders with similar profiles. As such, through this framework, it is not possible to predict the result of the whole peloton.

Another approach is to use past results to predict the outcome of a race [13]. This work focuses on predicting the mean stage velocity, the individual rider velocity, and the head-to-head wins for the Giro d'Italia, Vuelta a Espana, and Tour de France from 2016 to 2018 with an extensive set of features. The author used the results of the top 2018 Union Cycliste Internationale (UCI) cyclists (excluding team time trials). Features related to weather and the course of the race were also considered with a heavy feature engineering. By applying ML techniques the author obtained a MAE of 0.3758 m/s in the mean stage prediction and 0.4660 m/s in the individual rider velocity. As for the head-to-head win prediction, the author achieved an accuracy of 73.16%. Unfortunately, the author did not publish the prediction for the top 10 riders. For the head to head win a tree boosting algorithm has shown the best results.

3   Proposed Framework

In this section, we present a framework that aims to predict the outcome (i.e., final ranking) of a race. As shown in [4], many factors impact the performance of a rider. Consequently, considering all of the factors results in a very complex model. Here, we present a starting point that will be gradually increased in complexity over time. Figure 2 shows a general outline of the framework. Next, we will highlight the details and features of both the data and the framework.

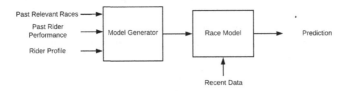

Fig. 2. Outline of the proposed framework

3.1   Past Relevant Races

In professional road cycling, many races are done in blocks where the same riders build up until the most important race(s). One example is the classical season where there is the following sequence: Omloop Het Nieuwsblad, Milano-San Remo, E3 Harelbeke (renamed to E3 BinckBank Classic), Tour of Flanders, and Paris-Roubaix. Another example is the sequence Critérium du Dauphiné, Tour de Suisse, and Tour de France. For our experiment we hand picked the relevant races.

3.2   Past Rider Performance

For each of the past races, it is important to measure the performance of the rider, as this can be a predictor for the result. For our experiment the relative time of completion (with the respect to the winner) has been used the performance metric.

3.3   Rider Profile

In order to account for overall rider performance (beyond the selected races), features from the rider profiles are also important. During races, unpredictable events can happen (for example, a malfunctioning bike or a crash) that can highly impact on the performance feature. Despite this unpredictable event, a rider can still have a good performance on the course. The rider profile can be defined by overall career points, career points from the previous year, and career points earned on similar races. A profile could also be traced by using more advanced features that take into account data from training and performance on different terrain, segment types.

3.4   Algorithm

As discussed in Sect. 2, different experiments have been conducted using a number of algorithms. In most of the cases, methods relying on NN have similar performance to other methods, as the datasets are not large enough for training a deep layered network. On the other hand, Boosting Tree algorithms in most cases showed the best results. As such, based on this assessment and our previous experience, we selected XGBoost for our framework. It was selected due to its ability to deal with missing values, speed, and accuracy [5,6]. As the missing values in the past race performance can happen for a number of unrelated reasons, we cannot impute them. Therefore, the chosen algorithm needs to deal with missing values, which is the case of XGBoost.

4   Case Study Description

For the case study, we have chosen to predict the results of the 2018 and 2019 editions of the Tour of Flanders. We have selected this race as it is one of the most important races in the classic season. Furthermore, the races in the classics block have maintained a large consistency over the years, leading to a more structured and consisted dataset.

4.1 Dataset Description

Data from the editions of 2008 to 2016 was used to train our model and to predict the results in 2018 and 2019. The entire dataset was scraped from Pro Cycling Stats (PCS). As the race performance feature, we used the relative finish time of the following races: Omloop Het Nieuwsblad, Strade Bianche, Milano-San Remo, E3 Harelbeke and Paris-Roubaix. We have chosen to use the relative time, as it is the best value that can indicate the relative performance in a race. The absolute time would change if there was any change in the weather or course. If we would use the ranking, there could be a big gap between the ranking while the performance in the race is similar. Such example is the Omloop Het Nieuwsblad 2018, where the riders from the 2nd to the 55th place arrived in the same group with the same relative time.

Furthermore, the riders that did not finish a certain race, were marked as missing value, as there could be any number of reasons for not completing a race. The rider profile was represented by the career points, sprint race points (as defined by PCS), and one-day race points. This is because the Tour of Flanders is categorized as a sprint race and one-day race by PCS. To represent the rider's experience over both the long and short team, the points from both the previous year and an Exponential Moving Average (EMA) over the last 10 years were considered.

Besides the rider's personal profile, the team of the rider also an impact, as some teams will have more experience (e.g., in terms of recruiting, preparation, and specific races) or might have better riders in their ranks. Therefore, we also considered the rider's team points from the previous year.

A very simple data cleaning step was performed: The riders that did not finish Tour of Flanders were excluded for that year from the data. Any rider with the total score below 60 PCS points in the previous year were also removed. A total of 544 data points were used. The final feature set is described in the Table 1.

5 Results and Discussion

After training the model and fitting the year 2018 and 2019, the resulting table was ordered by the predicted relative time that it took for a rider to complete the race. As such, we can also extract the predicted position in the race. The results, compared to the actual outcome, can be found in Table 2. For 2018 the model correctly predicted 2 riders out of the top 3 and 6 out of the top 10. However, for the 2019 edition, the model did not predict any riders from the top 3 and only 4 out of the top 10.

In order to further access the performance of our model, we compare it to human predictions (based on experience and domain knowledge). Therefore, we

Table 1. Description of the dataset

Feature type	Period considered	# of data points
Omloop het Nieuwsblad rel. time	Current year	340
Omloop het Nieuwsblad rel. time	Previous year	331
Strade Bianche rel. time	Current year	100
Strade Bianche rel. time	Previous year	83
Milano Sanremo rel. time	Current year	298
Milano Sanremo rel. time	Previous year	251
E3 Harelbeke rel. time	Current year	325
E3 Harelbeke rel. time	Previous year	263
Ronde van Vlaanderen rel. time	Previous year	362
Paris Roubaix rel. time	Previous year	319
Career Points	10 year EMA	544
Career Points	Current season until the race	544
One Day Race Points	10 year EMA	544
One Day Race Points	Current season until the race	544
Sprint Race Points	10 year EMA	544
Sprint Race Points	Current season until the race	544
Team Points	Previous year	544

compare our results in Table 3 with the collective picks from fans on the PCS website. In particular, we compare the number of riders that were picked out correctly by our model and the number of riders that were most picked out by the fans (a total of approximately 4000 fans voted).

We observe that for 2018 most of the metrics are better predicted by our model rather than by the fans. In contrast, for 2019, the metrics are more in favour of the fans. However, note that the accuracy of predictions is very low for to the 2019 edition. This is explained by the race events, where most candidate winners and teams were riding against each other (preventing somebody else to win), rather than trying to win themselves. As such, the outcome was very unexpected. In the previous work, it was shown that some team sports have a very large unpredictability factor. This proves to be true for road cycling and explains the lower performance in 2019.

Additionally, we investigated the importance of the considered features. Figure 3 shows that the model gives the most importance to the previous editions of the Omloop Het Nieuwsblad and the Tour of Flanders. In general, the average points also have a bigger importance. It's important to note that the feature importance is represented by the weight in this case, that is, how many times does that feature is used to split the data. However, this does not represent the whole picture. By looking at the SHapley Additive exPlanations (SHAP) values [10], we can see that the features that are the biggest contributors towards a

Table 2. Prediction for Tour of Flanders 2018 and 2019

Year	Name	Predicted rank	Actual rank	Predicted rel. time	Relative time
2018	Niki Terpstra	1	1	17	0
	Philippe Gilbert	2	3	41.4	17
	Arnaud Demare	3	15	51.4	73
	Daniel Oss	4	26	57.7	196
	Greg van Avermaet	5	5	62.6	25
	Sep Vanmarcke	6	13	67.9	25
	Gianni Moscon	7	21	70.5	73
	Peter Sagan	8	6	74.1	25
	Jasper Stuyven	9	7	75.9	25
	Tiesj Benoot	10	8	78.5	25
2019	Zdenek Stybar	1	36	13.3	140
	Greg van Avermaet	2	10	30.5	17
	Wout van Aert	3	14	31.2	17
	Tiesj Benoot	4	9	51.8	17
	Alexander Kristoff	5	3	53.8	17
	Oliver Naesen	6	7	54	17
	Matteo Trentin	7	21	68.6	118
	Yves Lampaert	8	17	80.8	17
	Peter Sagan	9	11	82.5	17
	Jasper Stuyven	10	19	83.7	79

Table 3. Prediction for Tour of Flanders 2018 and 2019

Metric	Model 2018	Fans 2018	Model 2019	Fans 2019
Top 3 in 3	2	0	0	0
Top 3 in 5	2	1	1	0
Top 3 in 10	2	2	1	1
Top 5 in 5	3	2	1	1
Top 5 in 10	3	3	1	2
Top 10 in 10	6	7	4	5

certain prediction. As an example, we look into the races towards Niki Terpstra's prediction (the actual and predicted winner of the 2018 edition). We observe, as seen in Fig. 4, that besides the 10 year one-day race points average and the one-day race points from the current year, the 2017 and 2018 editions of the E3 Harelbeke race have the largest contribution into the prediction for the Tour of Flanders. This example thus demonstrates that even though the model splits a lot on the result of the Omloop het Nieuwsblad, a good result in a lower importance-scored feature can still mean a higher ranking in the prediction of the race under consideration.

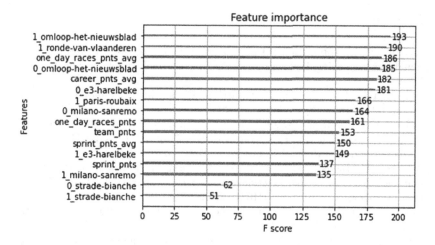

Fig. 3. Model feature importance

Fig. 4. SHAP value for the first ranked in 2018

6   Conclusions and Future Work

In this paper, we propose a framework for predicting the results of cycling races. In order to validate the viability of this framework, we opted for the Tour of Flanders as a case study and predicted the race results for the editions of 2018 and 2019. We show that a ML model can obtain a similar, or even higher, accuracy as human experts. As such, we showcase the potential of ML in this area and provide a starting point for future work.

For future work, we will enrich our dataset (by including, among others, weather information, sensor data, key segments, etc.) and perform additional feature engineering on the performance result (e.g., incorporating other (smaller) race). The challenge afterwards is to generalize this framework to other one-day races and also to multi-stage races, including Tour of France.

Acknowledgment. This work was partly funded by the DAIQUIRI project, cofunded by imec, a research institute founded by the Flemish Government. Project partners are Ghent University, InTheRace, Arinti, Cronos, VideoHouse, NEP Belgium, and VRT, with project support from VLAIO.

References

1. Karetnikov, A.: Application of Data-Driven Analytics on Sport Data from a Professional Bicycle Racing Team. Eindhoven University of Technology, The Netherlands (2019)
2. Alfredo, Y.F., Isa, S.M.: Football match prediction with tree based model classification. Int. J. Intell. Syst. Appl. **11**, 20–28 (2019)
3. Aoki, R.Y.S., Assunção, R., de Melo, P.O.S.V.: Luck is hard to beat: the difficulty of sports prediction. In: Proceedings of the 23rd ACM SIGKDD International Conference on Knowledge Discovery and Data Mining (2017)
4. Atkinson, G., Davison, R., Jeukendrup, A., Passfield, L.: Science and cycling: current knowledge and future directions for research. J. Sports Sci. **21**, 767–787 (2003). https://doi.org/10.1080/0264041031000102097
5. Bentéjac, C., Csörgo, A., Martínez-Muñoz, G.: A comparative analysis of XGBoost. ArXiv abs/1911.01914 (2019)
6. Chen, T., Guestrin, C.: XGBoost: a scalable tree boosting system. In: Proceedings of the 22nd ACM SIGKDD International Conference on Knowledge Discovery and Data Mining (2016)
7. Fried, G., Mumcu, C.: Sport Analytics: A Data-Driven Approach to Sport Business and Management. Taylor & Francis, London (2016)
8. Hilmkil, A., Ivarsson, O., Johansson, M., Kuylenstierna, D., van Erp, T.: Towards machine learning on data from professional cyclists. In: Proceedings of the 12th World Congress on Performance Analysis of Sports, pp. 168–176. Faculty of Kinesiology, University of Zagreb, Opatija (2018)
9. Kataoka, Y., Gray, P.: Real-time power performance prediction in tour de France. In: Brefeld, U., Davis, J., Van Haaren, J., Zimmermann, A. (eds.) MLSA 2018. LNCS (LNAI), vol. 11330, pp. 121–130. Springer, Cham (2019). https://doi.org/10.1007/978-3-030-17274-9_10
10. Lundberg, S.M., Lee, S.I.: A unified approach to interpreting model predictions. In: Guyon, I., et al. (eds.) Advances in Neural Information Processing Systems, vol. 30, pp. 4765–4774. Curran Associates, Inc. (2017). http://papers.nips.cc/paper/7062-a-unified-approach-to-interpreting-model-predictions.pdf
11. Passfield, L., Hopker, J., Jobson, S., Friel, D., Zabala, M.: Knowledge is power: issues of measuring training and performance in cycling. J. Sports Sci. **35**, 1426–1434 (2016). https://doi.org/10.1080/02640414.2016.1215504
12. Revinskaya, A.: Predicting cycling performance from historical data (2019)
13. Spiegeleer, E.D.: Predicting cycling results using machine learning (2019)
14. Thabtah, F., Zhang, L., Abdelhamid, N.: NBA game result prediction using feature analysis and machine learning. Ann. Data Sci. **6**, 103–116 (2019)

Mining Marathon Training Data to Generate Useful User Profiles

Jakim Berndsen(✉), Barry Smyth, and Aonghus Lawlor

Insight Center for Data Analytics, University College Dublin, Dublin, Ireland
{jakim.berndsen,barry.smyth,aonghus.lawlor}@insight-centre.org

Abstract. In this work we generate user profiles from the raw activity data of over 12000 marathon runners. We demonstrate that these user profiles capture accurate representations of the fitness and training of a runner, and show that they are comparable to current methods used to predict marathon performance – many of which require many years of prior experience or expensive laboratory testing. We also briefly investigate how these user profiles can be used to help marathon runners in their training and race preparation when combined with current recommender systems approaches.

Keywords: Marathon running · Sports analytics · Feature engineering

1 Introduction

Over the past decades, marathons have become mass participation events, with the most popular races attracting over 40,000 runners annually. The proliferation of smart, GPS enabled devices has led to the generation of large amounts of data surrounding runners' marathon training and performance. Companies such as Strava, Trainingpeaks, and Runkeeper have used this data to help millions of runners remain active and become fitter. In recent years there has been a shift in how this data has been used. Traditionally these running apps helped runners by providing an array of historical analyses – training logs, personal records, etc. – but the use of such analyses to improve performance is limited. Some runners have dropped these systems because the feedback delivered was not considered actionable [32]. Instead, researchers have begun developing predictive models and recommender systems that are capable of helping marathon runners through personalised advice [3,4,17,28,33,36].

Predicting the finish times of marathon runners has been addressed on multiple occasions. In a systemic review focusing on marathon finish time prediction, 114 marathon prediction equations were identified [26]. Each of these equations can be broken down as using one (or more) of four types of data: 26 equations used anthropomorphic variables of a runner (age, height, BMI etc.), 67 used training variables, 49 used figures derived from laboratory testing, while 41 equations utilised previous race times of runners.

© Springer Nature Switzerland AG 2020
U. Brefeld et al. (Eds.): MLSA 2020, CCIS 1324, pp. 113–125, 2020.
https://doi.org/10.1007/978-3-030-64912-8_10

One of the earliest attempts of generating a model to determine race finish time was made by Peter Riegel in 1981 [31]. Riegel identified a relationship between the log of time taken and the log of the distance of an event and fit an exponential equation where finish time could be predicted using the finish time of another, shorter race. This equation was popularised by the magazine RunnersWorld and is still commonly used by runners to predict a finish time over the marathon distance. More recently, the limits of such a universal scaling equation have been shown [22] with greater specificity being required to be applicable to marathon runners across a wide range of abilities. Different methods have since been used to predict marathon time based on previous race times, with Hidden Markov Models [27], Matrix Completion [8,9] and Neural Networks [15] being utilised to address some of the limitations of the Riegel model. Additionally, a larger sample of previous races has been used to individualise the predictions with [40] utilising two previous, shorter races to predict marathon finish time. Similarity and neighbourhood-based approaches have also been used to predict marathon times based on runners' entire race histories [33–36].

Marathon training data has also been used to determine a runner's finish time. Average weekly training distance has been combined with previous race times to predict marathon performance [40]. Promising results were also demonstrated when fitting a linear regression model to the average training distance and average training pace from the final 8 weeks of marathon preparation [39]. While evaluating the training determinants of marathon performance, Doherty et al. [14] found 7 features to be particularly indicative of marathon finish time; mean weekly distance, number of weekly runs, number of long (>32 km) runs, longest training distance in a single week, distance of longest run, mean training pace, and weekly training duration.

Physiological features have also previously been used to determine marathon finish time. VO_2max [6,13], Lactate Threshold [19] and Critical Velocity [18] have demonstrated predictive ability. Physical variables such as body fat percentage [2,41] and BMI [23], alongside features such as age and gender, have also been used to develop predictive models.

While many of these methods provide reasonable predictive accuracy, they lack the ability to help recreational marathon runners. Laboratory testing is expensive and often beyond the scope of recreational runners. Models utilising previous finish time struggle to make accurate predictions for the marathon distance and often operate under the naive assumption that runners have the same level of fitness for the target race as they had previously. Equally, predictive models based on a runner's training have thus far required a full complement of training data to generate predictions. This makes them unhelpful and inaccurate until all training has been completed.

Despite the drawbacks of these models, many runners still use them to inform their training and preparation for the marathon. In this study, we aim to address these issues by generating user profiles for recreational marathon runners. These user profiles represent both the physiological fitness of a runner and a broad description of their marathon training. We will show that these user profiles are capable of accurately predicting finish time throughout various points of training and demonstrate how, alongside previous research, these user profiles can be used to help runners prepare for the marathon.

2   Generating User Profiles

We briefly describe the data utilised to generate user profiles. We use the training data of marathon runners who have run one of the London, New York, or Dublin marathons in the years 2014–2017. For each runner we have GPS data for every training session they have undertaken in the 16 weeks immediately preceding the race. The GPS data has been converted into pacing data (mins/km) and been sampled at 100 m intervals. We also have information on the corresponding race performance for this training data. In total, we have detailed data for over 650,000 training sessions, taken from 196,642 training weeks of 12,627 athletes. These runners completed the marathon with an average finish time of 235($\pm$34.5) minutes.

2.1   Fastest Pace Representation

Previous race times have been successful in predicting the finish times of marathon runners. One of the main drawbacks of this approach is that a runner must have run a recent race time while at a similar level of fitness to their current state. As runners' training tends to be geared towards a target race, and their fitness levels vary greatly based on the quantity of training being undertaken, this is an unrealistic approach to estimate a runner's ability during a training programme.

We note that runners run different types of sessions at varying intensities during their marathon preparation. While many sessions will simply comprise of accumulating distance, preparing runners for the physical demands of covering the race distance of 42.2 km, others (tempo, interval sessions etc.) will see athletes run for shorter distances at faster paces. As runners get fitter the speed at which they are capable of running these shorter distances increases. Despite the fact these sessions are rarely covered at maximal effort we postulate that these speeds could be used to approximate the race times over certain distances.

For each week of training we, therefore, calculate the fastest pace for a variety of distances by calculating the fastest pace that distance was covered in training. This is done by computing the minimum rolling mean pace for window lengths corresponding to distances of 3 km, 5 km, 10 km and 15 km as in Eq. 1, where d is the specified distance and n is the number of sessions run to date. The fastest pace is calculated for each week of training and corresponds to the fastest pace for each distance seen so far in training.

$$min\{rolling(\text{Paces}_i, d)\}_{i=1}^{n} \tag{1}$$

The distances of 3 km, 5 km, 10 km, and 15 km are chosen as target distances for this calculation; both because training programmes may push runners to run fast times at these distances (e.g. 10 km tempo runs). Equally, runners often participate in other races during marathon preparation and, as such, distances that are similar to common road race distances (5 km, 10 km, 10 miles) were chosen.

2.2 Mining Physiological Variables of Runners

As mentioned in the introduction of this paper, physiological variables have seen great success in predicting the finish time of marathon runners. While these variables largely rely on expensive laboratory testing, usually measured using specialised equipment, we examine ways to infer these features directly from raw marathon training data.

VO_2max is a common measure of fitness. It measures the maximal rate of oxygen consumption [29] and is normally measured during an incremental treadmill test using an oxygen mask [7]. VO_2max can, however, also be estimated from a maximal effort race pace using the Daniels formula [12]. We use each of the fastest paces calculated in Sect. 2.1 as a proxy for a maximal effort pace and use the Daniels formula to calculate a corresponding vO_2max at that pace and distance. The estimated vO_2max of a runner is then represented as the mean and standard deviation of these calculated vO_2max values.

Critical Speed (CS) describes the relationship between fatigue and exercise intensity; it is the highest intensity at which a physiological steady state can be reached [25,30]. The super-maximal distance represents a finite amount of exercise that can be run at speeds faster than CS. CS has been found to accurately describe both marathon performance and pacing in runners [37]. We again treat our fastest paces as approximations for maximal effort runs and treat the time taken as the time to exhaustion. We then calculate the CS and super-maximal distance of a runner using the equations described in [37].

In sports science, the lactate threshold is the maximal exercise effort that can be sustained for an extended period of time without an increase in blood lactate [5]. As with vO_2max, a runner's lactate threshold is measured using an incremental treadmill test though it is also possible to estimate lactate threshold using time trials. A related measure is *functional threshold pace* (FTP) - the fastest pace that can be sustained for a duration of 45–60 min. We calculate a runner's FTP using a method similar to our calculation of fastest paces. Instead of calculating a runner's fastest pace over various distances, we compute their FTP using their fastest pace over fixed durations. We generate FTP values corresponding to durations of 45, 50, 55, and 60 min.

Combining these physiological variables (vO_2max, CS, super-maximal distance, FTP) gives a physiological representation of a runner's level of fitness for every week of their marathon preparation. As marathon training progresses and runners' fitness levels increase, we would expect these values to improve.

2.3 Cumulative and Weekly Training Representation

We wish to generate a representation of marathon training that is capable of capturing the volume, intensity, and frequency of an athlete's training. We focus specifically on computing features from [14] that have been found to be particularly indicative of marathon performance. For each week of training completed, we calculate the following information on the cumulative pace, distance, and duration of training completed:

- The number of training sessions completed
- The mean and coefficient of variation of training pace
- The mean, variation, and maximum distance per session
- The mean, variation, and maximum distance per week
- The mean, variation, and maximum duration per session
- The mean, variation, and maximum duration per week
- The number of long (>32 km) runs completed
- The mean, variation, and maximum number of training sessions completed per week
- The proportion of distance run in each pace zones based on 45 min FTP

We note that average training pace is insufficient to fully capture training intensity as it gives no indication of how long a runner spent at different intensities. Running interval or tempo sessions alongside slower long runs should be represented differently to a runner that runs all their sessions at a constant pace. Pace zones have been used to define exercise intensity by categorising running pace into one of multiple intensity zones based on fixed percentage values of that runner's FTP [38]. We use a runner's 45 min FTP and the percentage thresholds used by TrainingPeaks[1] to determine the proportional distance run by a runner in each of 7 defined pace intensity zones.

While this representation captures cumulative information on all training completed so far, we also wish to capture a more short term representation of a runner's training. Marathon training plans follow a number of microcycles – several hard weeks of training to build fitness levels followed by rest to allow recovery and reduce injury risk - in a system known as periodisation [20,21]. The types of training conducted may differ between periodisation cycles – early training focusing on building general fitness while later cycles concentrate on training sessions more specifically directed at speeds and distances associated with the marathon. We, therefore, wish to represent these changes and capture more short term information on a runner's training to supplement the cumulative features generated above.

Rather than capturing a single week of marathon training, we note that periodisation cycles are generally 4 weeks in length. We therefore capture features for each individual week within this 4 week period - i.e 5 weeks before the marathon we compute features for the 6th, 7th, 8th, and 9th weeks before race day. For each training week, we record the following:

---

[1] https://www.trainingpeaks.com/blog/joe-friel-s-quick-guide-to-setting-zones/.

- The number of training sessions completed
- The mean and variation of pace in that week
- The mean, variation, and maximum distance of training sessions
- The mean, variation, and maximum duration of training sessions
- The cumulative distance/duration of all sessions
- The fastest 3 km/5 km/10 km paces during that week
- The proportion of distance run in each pace zone based on 45 min FTP

Each week is represented by 21 individual features. The features of individual weeks are concatenated to represent a training microcycle ($4 \times 21 = 84$ features).

We note that a potential problem of this approach is that runners may be out of sync with each other, running rest weeks at different times of their training programmes. We deal with this problem by sorting the weeks based on their total training distance. In our representation, $w-4$ represents the week with the most training volume, $w-3$ the second most etc. This approach proved effective in previous work using similar training representations [16]. This representation requires multiple weeks of previous training data and is therefore only computed for the final 12 training weeks.

These cumulative and periodised training features are combined with the fastest paces and physiological features of a runner to generate a final user profile. Each runner is associated with 12 user profiles each corresponding to one week of their marathon training. Each user profile is represented by 125 parameters.

3   Evaluation

To evaluate whether user profiles calculated from raw training data provide an accurate representation of a runner we use them to predict marathon finish times. We evaluated multiple regression algorithms to predict marathon finish times; Linear Regression, Elastic Nets, Bayesian Ridge Regression, Decision Trees, Random Forests, Gradient Boosting, and Neural Networks. We use 10-fold cross validation, ensuring that all training weeks from a single runner appear only within a single fold, to calculate the mean absolute error (MAE) and mean absolute percentage error (MAPE) of each method. For brevity, we include only the results of gradient boosting (implemented using XGBoost [11]) as, after experimentation, this was found to produce the lowest prediction errors.

3.1   Prediction Error in Training

We will evaluate four different representations of a runner's training, each one iteratively adding to the features of the previous: the fastest pace (FP) representation; FP with physiological variables (PV); PV with cumulative weekly features (CW); and CW with sorted, multiple week representation (MW). We make predictions for every runner in our dataset and compare overall and weekly errors between these representations.

The MW representation has the lowest prediction error of any representation with an MAE of 13.67 min (MAPE = 5.73%). This is a 2.18 min improvement

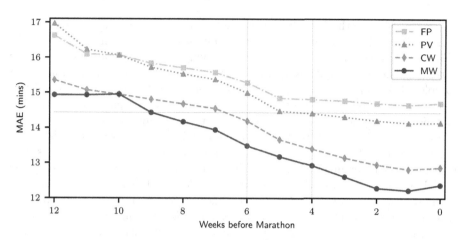

Fig. 1. The mean absolute percentage error (minutes) by week of marathon training using the FP, PV, CW and MW user profile representations.

over a baseline prediction using the FP representation, representing a 13.8% improvement in prediction accuracy. A comparison of the MAPE and MAE of each of our models can be seen in Table 1.

Table 1. A comparison of the MAE and MAPE for the different user profile representations

Model	MAE	MAPE
FP	15.85	6.65
PV	15.89	6.68
CW	14.38	6.03
MW	13.69	5.73

A comparison with previous systems suggests that our MW user profiles are accurate enough to be useful in practice. Our user profiles exhibit a MAPE of just 5.16% (MAE = 12.35 min) on the day preceding the target race. This compares favourably to the errors presented in current state of the art systems [26], many of which require advanced laboratory testing to generate accurate predictions. The Riegel Formula [31], which is still commonly used, has seen prediction errors of approximately 10% when used to predict the marathon finish times of recreational athletes [3]. Additionally, the MAPE of 5.73%, calculated across all previous weeks of marathon training, suggests that the generated user profiles provide good predictive accuracy throughout all stages of marathon preparation. This is preferable to other methods that require full complements of training data or recent testing to ensure accuracy. Indeed, using the final 8 weeks of training pace and distance information allows us to generate a finish time prediction as in [39]. This method predicts marathon finish time with an error of 8.78% (MAE=21.2 mins) when using the same runners as presented in this paper. Our MW user profiles are capable of almost halving the prediction error made by current methods utilising training data after all marathon preparation has been completed. We also note that each of our representations is capable of outperforming this system even in the early weeks of marathon preparation, a situation in which this method is incapable of producing a prediction.

As we wish our user profiles to be able to predict marathon finish time throughout marathon preparation, we investigate how the error changes as runners progress through their training. The MAE for predictions in each of the final 12 weeks of training is depicted in Fig. 1. We see that, for each of our representations, the error decreases as training progresses. This is to be expected - future training is an unknown in our user profile meaning it should be easier to predict finish time when there is less uncertainty in this regard. Equally, the fitness and training representation is likely to become more accurate over time as it encapsulates more information.

Figure 1 also clearly shows the benefit of the additional features in our representation, with larger representations capable of making more accurate predictions earlier in the training plan. While MW and CW closely match each other in the early stages of training, we see MW begin to significantly outperform CW 9 weeks before the marathon - likely the point that training intensity and volume during periodised microcycles diverges from prior training. The prediction error of 14.43 min using the MW profile cannot be bettered by CW until 6 weeks before the marathon; it takes a further 2 weeks for the PV representation to predict at this level of accuracy while FP never comes close.

The aim, in the future, is to use these user profiles as a basis to make training and pacing recommendations to marathon runners. We, therefore, want a representation capable of depicting a runner's fitness and training as early as possible, such that tailored recommendations can be made to a runner early enough for them to be taken advantage of. The fact that MW is capable of making accurate predictions so much earlier than the other representations, and has high predictive accuracy throughout marathon preparation, gives us confidence that this MW user profile would prove useful for such a purpose.

3.2   Error - Age, Gender and Ability

We wish to examine the relationship between finish time prediction error – as an approximation of user profile accuracy – and age, gender, and ability of runners. We analyse the errors generated by our MW representation in the final week of training based on the finish time, as well as gender (male or female) and age (over-40 and under-40). The predictions errors, split into cohorts based on gender and age, can be seen in Figs. 2 and 3.

We see a strong relationship between finish time and the prediction error generated from our MW representation. We note that the most accurate predictions are made for faster runners, with accuracy beginning to decline in finish times significantly slower than 240 min. This mimics the effects reported by [3] when

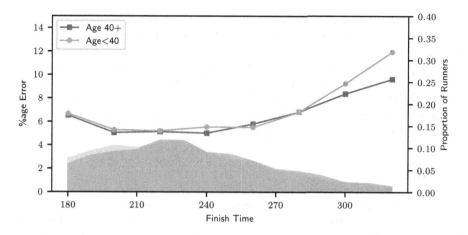

Fig. 2. The percentage error by age of runners as finish times progress. Also shown is a distribution of finish times by each cohort.

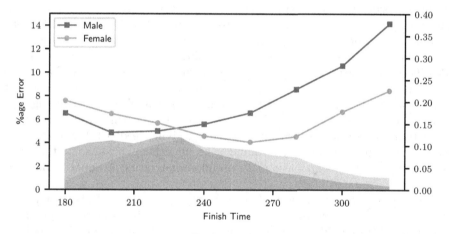

Fig. 3. The percentage error by gender of runners as finish times progress. Also shown is a distribution of finish times by each cohort.

investigating previous-race time prediction approaches. Some of this effect may be due to the types of training undertaken by runners. Faster runners may be more likely to follow a structured training plan and may, therefore, be following more similar patterns of training. In contrast, the times run by slower runners may be achievable through a considerably less structured approach, leading to relatively dissimilar training plans and an increased prediction error. We also note that there are fewer runners for slower finish times, creating fewer training examples, and therefore some of this increased error may be alleviated by including a greater number of slow runners in our analysis.

Previous research has suggested that males may be more likely to run the marathon with inadequate preparation [24]. We therefore expect this lack of preparation to be reflected by a less representative user profile for male runners, especially those running slower finish times. Figure 3 suggests that this is indeed the case. The model predicts finish time with significantly lower errors for female runners; particularly in runners finishing slower than 4 h. This is despite female runners making up only 25% of our dataset. On the other hand, age exhibits no significant effect on the predictive accuracy of our user profile.

4   Discussion

A key contribution of this work has been to generate an accurate representation of both a runner's current fitness levels and previous training. These user profiles can be used to predict the finish times of runners. This contribution has the potential of having an impact on the preparation of marathon runners. Recommender systems have previously been generated that recommend individualised training sessions to marathon runners [17,28]. Through the use of a more accurate user profile, training sessions can be recommended that better reflect the current abilities of a runner. This can be used to ensure that training sessions are achievable to a runner, or to recommend training that targets a specific weakness identified in the user profile. We have also shown that our user profiles have good predictive accuracy at all points in marathon training. This a positive contrast to previous methods, such as [39], that require a full complement of training data to make an accurate prediction. This means that accurate marathon finish time predictions can be made throughout training, giving feedback to runners and letting them know their current training is keeping them on course for their goal time. Such predictions may also prove useful in motivating a runner throughout training.

An equally important part of marathon preparation is devising a pacing strategy; a plan of how to divide one's effort efficiently to avoid fatigue later in the race. Case-based reasoning and previous race times have previously been used to tackle this problem [34,35]. The use of an accurate user profile can lead to the selection of better cases, while a more accurate finish time prediction can lead to a strategy being devised for a more realistic target time.

In [4], recommendations are made to influence runner behaviour during the running of their marathon. If a runner is considered at risk of fatiguing before the end of the marathon an altered pacing strategy is presented mid-race. This intervention aims to help marathon runners fend off early fatigue, thereby ensuring a faster finish by avoiding the detrimental effects *hitting the wall* can have on race performance. An accurate representation of a runner's physiological condition and training would help such a system identify fatigue at earlier stages of the race, allowing for earlier and smaller interventions to be made.

The user profiles presented in this work rely on pacing data only. In recent years, heart rate monitors have become ubiquitous in running watches, giving a further set of features to add to a user profile. From an investigation of our data, it appears that this trend was only beginning in the latter stages of the period of data collection, with only a small proportion (<15%) recording heart rate throughout the entirety of their training. Therefore, the decision was made not to include heart rate in our analysis. Nonetheless, encoding information on heart rate, such as maximum heart rate, heart rate zones [10], or TRIMP scores [1] would likely improve the representation of both physical fitness and training in our user profiles, and is therefore the logical extension to the work presented here.

5 Conclusion

We have described techniques for generating user profiles that capture both physiological and training information. We have shown that these user profiles provide accurate estimates of a runner's ability through their capacity to accurately predict marathon finish time throughout training. In our discussion, we looked at how these user profiles can be used to improve performance by informing runners on training and pacing decisions through the use of a variety of pre-existing recommender systems.

Acknowledgements. This work is supported by the Insight Centre for Data Analytics under Grant Number SFI/12/RC/2289_P2.

References

1. Banister, E., Banister, E., Banister, E., Banister, E.: Modeling elite athletic performance. Human Kinetics (1991)
2. Barandun, U., et al.: Running speed during training and percent body fat predict race time in recreational male marathoners. Open Access J. Sports Med. **3**, 51 (2012)
3. Berndsen, J., Lawlor, A., Smyth, B.: Running with recommendation. In: HealthRecSys@ RecSys. pp. 18–21 (2017)
4. Berndsen, J., Smyth, B., Lawlor, A.: Pace my race: recommendations for marathon running. In: Proceedings of the 13th ACM Conference on Recommender Systems. pp. 246–250 (2019)
5. Billat, V., Bernard, O., Pinoteau, J., Petit, B., Koralsztein, J.: Time to exhaustion at vo2max and lactate steady state velocity in sub elite long-distance runners. Archives internationales de physiologie, de biochimie et de biophysique **102**(3), 215–219 (1994)
6. Billat, V.L., Demarle, A., Slawinski, J., Paiva, M., Koralsztein, J.P.: Physical and training characteristics of top-class marathon runners. Med. Sci. Sports Exercise **33**(12), 2089–2097 (2001)
7. Billat, V., Hill, D., Pinoteau, J., Petit, B., Koralsztein, J.P.: Effect of protocol on determination of velocity at vo2 max and on its time to exhaustion. Arch. Physiol. Biochem. **104**(3), 313–321 (1996)
8. Blythe, D.A., Király, F.J.: Prediction and quantification of individual athletic performance. arXiv preprint arXiv:1505.01147 (2015)

9. Blythe, D.A., Király, F.J.: Prediction and quantification of individual athletic performance of runners. PLoS ONE **11**(6), e0157257 (2016)
10. Burke, E.: Precision heart rate training. Human Kinetics (1998)
11. Chen, T., Guestrin, C.: XGBoost: A scalable tree boosting system. In: Proceedings of the 22nd ACM SIGKDD International Conference on Knowledge Discovery and Data Mining. pp. 785–794. KDD 2016, ACM, New York, USA (2016)
12. Daniels, J.: Daniels' running formula. Human Kinetics (2013)
13. Di Prampero, P., Atchou, G., Brückner, J.C., Moia, C.: The energetics of endurance running. Eur. J. Appl. Physiol. **55**(3), 259–266 (1986)
14. Doherty, C., Keogh, A., Davenport, J., Lawlor, A., Smyth, B., Caulfield, B.: An evaluation of the training determinants of marathon performance: a meta-analysis with meta-regression. J. Sci. Med. Sport **23**(2), 182–188 (2020)
15. Dracopoulos, D.C.: A better predictor of marathon race times based on neural networks. In: Bramer, M., Petridis, M. (eds.) SGAI 2017. LNCS (LNAI), vol. 10630, pp. 293–299. Springer, Cham (2017). https://doi.org/10.1007/978-3-319-71078-5_25
16. Feely, C., Caulfield, B., Lawlor, A., Smyth, B.: Using case-based reasoning to predict marathon performance and recommend tailored training plans. In: Watson, I., Weber, R. (eds.) ICCBR 2020. LNCS (LNAI), vol. 12311, pp. 67–81. Springer, Cham (2020). https://doi.org/10.1007/978-3-030-58342-2_5
17. Fister Jr., I., Fister, I.: Generating the training plans based on existing sports activities using swarm intelligence. In: Patnaik, S., Yang, X.-S., Nakamatsu, K. (eds.) Nature-Inspired Computing and Optimization. MOST, vol. 10, pp. 79–94. Springer, Cham (2017). https://doi.org/10.1007/978-3-319-50920-4_4
18. Florence, S.I., Weir, J.P.: Relationship of critical velocity to marathon running performance. Euro. J. Appl. Physiol. Occup. Physiol. **75**(3), 274–278 (1997)
19. Föhrenbach, R., Mader, A., Hollmann, W.: Determination of endurance capacity and prediction of exercise intensities for training and competition in marathon runners. Int. J. Sports Med. **8**(01), 11–18 (1987)
20. Fry, R.W., Morton, A.R., Keast, D.: Periodisation and the prevention of overtraining. Canad. J. Sport Sci.= J. canadien des sciences du sport **17**(3), 241–248 (1992)
21. Fry, R.W., Morton, A.R., Keast, D.: Periodisation of training stress-a review. Canad. J. Sport Sci. = Journal canadien des sciences du sport **17**(3), 234–240 (1992)
22. García-Manso, J., Martín-González, J., Vaamonde, D., Da Silva-Grigoletto, M.: The limitations of scaling laws in the prediction of performance in endurance events. J. Theor. Biol. **300**, 324–329 (2012)
23. Hagan, R., Upton, S., Duncan, J., Gettman, L.: Marathon performance in relation to maximal aerobic power and training indices in female distance runners. Br. J. Sports Med. **21**(1), 3–7 (1987)
24. Hubble, C., Zhao, J.: Gender differences in marathon pacing and performance prediction. J. Sports Anal. **2**(1), 19–36 (2016)
25. Jones, A.M., Burnley, M., Black, M.I., Poole, D.C., Vanhatalo, A.: The maximal metabolic steady state: redefining the 'gold standard'. Physiological Reports **7**(10), e14098 (2019)
26. Keogh, A., Smyth, B., Caulfield, B., Lawlor, A., Berndsen, J., Doherty, C.: Prediction equations for marathon performance: a systematic review. Int. J. Sports Physiol. Perform. **14**(9), 1159–1169 (2019)
27. Millett, M., Melanson, T.: Predicting running times from race history (2015)

28. Mohan, S., Venkatakrishnan, A., Silva, M., Pirolli, P.: On designing a social coach to promote regular aerobic exercise. In: Twenty-Ninth IAAI Conference (2017)
29. Noakes, T.: Lore of running. Human Kinetics (2003)
30. Poole, D.C., Burnley, M., Vanhatalo, A., Rossiter, H.B., Jones, A.M.: Critical power: an important fatigue threshold in exercise physiology. Med. Sci. Sports Exerc. **48**(11), 2320 (2016)
31. Riegel, P.S.: Athletic records and human endurance: A time vs. distance equation describing world-record performances may be used to compare the relative endurance capabilities of various groups of people. Am. Sci. **69**(3), 285–290 (1981)
32. Schneider, H.: Adapting at run-time: Exploring the design space of personalized fitness coaches. In: Proceedings of the 22nd International Conference on Intelligent User Interfaces Companion, pp. 173–176 (2017)
33. Smyth, B.: Marathon race planning: A case-based reasoning approach. In: The 27th International Joint Conference on Artificial Intelligence (IJCAI 2018), Stockholm, Sweden, 13–19 July (2018)
34. Smyth, B., Cunningham, P.: A novel recommender system for helping marathoners to achieve a new personal-best. In: Proceedings of the Eleventh ACM Conference on Recommender Systems, pp. 116–120 (2017)
35. Smyth, B., Cunningham, P.: Running with cases: a cbr approach to running your best marathon. In: Aha, D.W., Lieber, J. (eds.) ICCBR 2017. LNCS (LNAI), vol. 10339, pp. 360–374. Springer, Cham (2017). https://doi.org/10.1007/978-3-319-61030-6_25
36. Smyth, B., Cunningham, P.: An analysis of case representations for marathon race prediction and planning. In: Cox, M.T., Funk, P., Begum, S. (eds.) ICCBR 2018. LNCS (LNAI), vol. 11156, pp. 369–384. Springer, Cham (2018). https://doi.org/10.1007/978-3-030-01081-2_25
37. Smyth, B., Muniz-Pumares, D.: Calculation of critical speed from raw training data in recreational marathon runners. Medicine and Science in Sports and Exercise (2020)
38. Stöggl, T.L., Sperlich, B.: The training intensity distribution among well-trained and elite endurance athletes. Front. Physiol. **6**, 295 (2015)
39. Tanda, G.: Prediction of marathon performance time on the basis of training indices. J. Human Sport Exerc., 511–520 (2011)
40. Vickers, A.J., Vertosick, E.A.: An empirical study of race times in recreational endurance runners. BMC Sports Sci. Med. Rehab. **8**(1), 26 (2016)
41. Zillmann, T., Knechtle, B., Rüst, C.A., Knechtle, P., Rosemann, T., Lepers, R.: Comparison of training and anthropometric characteristics between recreational male half-marathoners and marathoners. Chin. J. Physiol. **56**(3), 138–146 (2013)

Learning from Partially Labeled Sequences for Behavioral Signal Annotation

Anna Aniszewska-Stępień[1,2(✉)], Romain Hérault[1], Guillaume Hacques[2], Ludovic Seifert[2], and Gilles Gasso[1]

[1] INSA Rouen Normandy, Saint-Ètienne-du-Rouvray, France
`anna.aniszewska@insa-rouen.fr`
[2] Rouen University Normandy, Mont-Saint-Aignan, France

Abstract. Herewith, we present a learning procedure that allows to deal with a partially labeled sequence dataset, i.e. when each sequence in the train dataset may contain labeled as well as unlabeled chunks. In our application case, this occurs when motor activity has been manually annotated (due to the recognition based on the video recording) and independently registered by the measuring system of high precision (touch sensors): human annotation misses some events that have been captured by the sensors. In the general setting, we aim at predicting the labels for a new fully unlabeled movement sequence, while the training has been performed on the partially labeled dataset. For this purpose we propose to use classical sequence model (hidden Markov model) that is furnished with a constrained Viterbi algorithm, which gives us a quick access to the *hard* approximation of the correct labeling sequences. We demonstrate, that this simple modification that constrained Viterbi provide, allows the HMM model to be trained on sparse data, and overall results in surprisingly high log-likelihood and accuracy level in annotating the partially labeled behavioral sequences in climbing. The same time we show the way to access correct labeling of the unannotated signal that can be helpful in various sport science studies for movement pattern sequential prediction.

Keywords: Partially labeled data · Hidden Markov model · Constrained viterbi algorithm · Behavioral signal labeling · Climbing pattern discovery

1 Introduction

In the real word, we very rarely posses the full information about the environment. For a machine learning prediction task, in the ideal setting, we shall dispose reliable and fully described data to train the model for pattern prediction in the newly observed data set; whereas this condition is hardly ever met in practice. Even for the experimental training data set, there can be missing information due to the errors or gaps in annotation, especially if the large information set is labeled by human and/or the labels are not not trivially accessed. Depending on the type of data (discrete or continuous) and the suspected distributions of labels, there can be different approaches to solve this problem.

© Springer Nature Switzerland AG 2020
U. Brefeld et al. (Eds.): MLSA 2020, CCIS 1324, pp. 126–139, 2020.
https://doi.org/10.1007/978-3-030-64912-8_11

In this type of tasks (e.g.. behavioral signal annotation, entity recognition, protein structure recognition), we want to label the observation sequences with a respective sequences that consist of the finite set of labels. Furthermore, the provided training sequences have some labels missing, while the missing ratio vary from sample to sample. Thus, all our training sequences may be partially labeled, but we still need to build a model that fully annotates the validation/test unlabeled sequences.

Proposed Approach. In the following article we will study a generative model that has been usually used in the context of sequential learning [8] adjusted to learn on sparsely labeled sequences. Namely, we will construct the procedure for the hidden Markov model to be learned from the sequences with voids in annotation, thanks to the Viterbi algorithm, that is modified in a way to find the optimal path passing by few constrained, known states. The proposed algorithm learns the distribution of the states with hidden Markov model and uses constrained Viterbi algorithm to predict the missing labels in the sequences; iteration over these two steps until convergence, emerges the stable sequence labeling close to the true one, which has been evaluated herewith in terms of log-likelihood and similarity (accuracy) ratio. We will show, how this relatively simple approach, resolves complex task, that is frequently encountered when we dispose only very little knowledge about the observation states. Our analysis aims at proving the efficiency of the proposed approach within the task of labeling the observation behavioral signal for which we never access the full information about the proper labels (not even for the training data sample). This situation is potentially frequently present in sport, when the access to the whole range of annotation is difficult and expensive (in terms of time and expert knowledge), while we need to draw generalized knowledge about the patterns present in large data sets, which as in our case, are registered time series. The motor task that produced the signal of our interest is the relative climber's position on the wall in the moment of touching the hold. The state (label) that we would like to find, is the kind of limb used for the support. The so obtained designation is crucial to find climbers profiles in the skill acquisition patterns discovery [3]. We suppose however, that the proposed approach in the same way may be applied to design the patterns of subjects' strategy during any other motor task.

Article Structure. The paper is organized as follows. After introducing the state-of-the-art (Sect. 2), we illustrate the context in which the model has been tested and provide the characteristics of the model (Sect. 3). Then, in Sect. 4, we detail the model and the adjustments for partial learning. The experiments and evaluation methods for the results are defined in Section 5. Next, we specify the type of evaluation used and finally we interpret the results and conclude (Sect. 6).

2   Related Work

Research works using both labelled and unlabeled data for training have mostly considered the classical case of semi-supervised learning in which each sequence example is either fully labeled or fully unlabeled [5]. The techniques that are used for semi-supervised sequential learning (within the broader area of structural learning) are multiple and deeply studied (mostly in the framework of NLP) over a number of recent years (e.g. deep learning models with pre-training word vectors [14] or self-training [6,7], co-training [2], conditional random fields [19] and many other). We would like to however insist in the distinction of the above mentioned situation from the one we study in the present article: we here address observable sequences which are incompletely annotated, in which the presence of gaps and voids within each sequence reduce the labelling ratio (that is 1 for fully labelled sequence). Notwithstanding thus obtained *partially* labeled data sets are omnipresent, the situation of scarce access to the experimental data for sequential learning, has not yet been extensively explored in the literature.

One known discriminative approach to address this challenge has been proposed by Fernandes and Brefeld [9]. They used structured perceptron furnished with Viterbi algorithm to cope with the non-labeled parts of the sequences. This allows them to train the perceptron on only the labelled parts of the sequences. Thus obtained model (simple transductive loss-augmented perceptron, STLAP), in spite of its simplicity, results in proper annotation for the initial labeling ratio larger than 0.5, which is comparable with standard supervised or semi-supervised methods. Also, in [10] the hidden Markov model with Baum-Welch algorithm has been compared by the same authors to the above mentioned STLAP in the partial training framework (see also [18]). The distinction with our approach however is that in our contribution we apply constrained Viterbi to even simpler model (hidden Markov model), for which we claim very good label annotation level. A separate branch of research employs conditional random fields, for example in Li *et al.* [13] different learning models are trained and subsequently combined for large scale sequential learning by adapting the idea of ensemble training. The result obtained on some types of partially labeled data were comparable to basic conditional random field approach, however the concept of many learning models may not be applicable to some type of data, especially when the transition between the tokens in the sequence is crucial as in our case. Conditional random fields combined with deep learning has been also recently studied in [22] in order to learn with annotation of various degrees (unsupervised, fully supervised and partially labeled sequences) in a unified way. Surprisingly, almost all the above mentioned papers claimed that the outcomes received for the partially labeled training data result in comparable performance or even outperform the ones received for the fully labeled data set (as they may avoid overfitting). Even though we do not study this property in the present article, some detailed studies of the phenomenon have been presented in [15] and [21]. Due to this fact and facing costly annotations of partially labeled data, there is a growing number of publications in the field, as for example the recent experiments in combining contradictory partial annotations from different datasets conduced by Huang *et al.* [12]. Additionally, and given that the above models have been tested the data only empirically, the required statistical consistency justification for the published discriminative models used for structural learning has been provided by Antoniuk *et al.* in [1].

3   Application Context

The partially labeled learning has been studied mostly for the linguistic tasks (entity recognition, natural language processing) or biological sequence analysis (protein structure, DNA sequences). Our application in sport science requires to work on the behavioral signal that is difficult to be systematically processed due to its innate complexity and its spatio-temporal continuous nature. For a sport science application later purpose (climbers' patterns discovery, as in [3]), we study the following case. The climbing data (mass center position combined with handhold touch time of the climber while moving up the artificial wall, Fig. 1(a)) is recorded by a camera (for the mass center) and, separately, by the wall sensors (for hold touch time). Hold touches that are visible on the video recording have been manually annotated by which kind of foot or hand (left hand, right hand, left foot, right foot) performs the action. Naturally, so obtained labeling contains a lot of voids as part of the events recorded by the hold sensors are not present or hidden in the video used by human for annotating. Meanwhile, the manual annotation has been rendered only for a subset of the recordings.

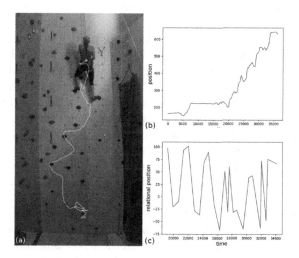

Fig. 1. (a) Experimental setting for climbing of the artificial wall (the mass-center trajectory of the climber is marked with the yellow line). The signal is composed by the time train of the distance between the climber's hip and limb position, when touching the hold. Different types of climbing routes and training paradigms have been used all along the data collection protocol. (b) Position of climber's body center collapsed to 1D by summation $(x + y)$ - evolution in time. (c) Observation signal as the relative position of the body centre vs the limb that is touching the hold (collapsed to 1D by summation).

Since human annotation is very costly (it requires expert knowledge and is time consuming) and at the same time - as being based on the visual attribution

- it is not precise, hence we face two challenges simultaneously: 1) the labeling does not cover the whole set of experimentally collected recordings and 2) annotations do carry the mistakes or gaps in the describing sequences. Thus, dealing with these both difficulties (as well as with possible noise) is not a trivial task. One another difficulty we encounter when annotating only subset of the recordings, is the supposed difference in the distributions between the annotated and the unannotated set. Due to the climbing learning protocol evolution, the sequences were not stationary, Fig. 2. The protocol (as explained in [11]) consisted in thirteen climbing sessions: three test sessions and ten training sessions. The test sessions aimed at scanning the behavioral repertoire of the participants. More specifically, to assess to what extent the participants could perform hand alternations (i.e., they used the two different hands on two subsequent movements) and hand repetitions (i.e., they used the same hand on two subsequent movements). In this purpose, they had to climb three different routes that either encouraged to perform alternations, repetitions or both coordination patterns (i.e., the Neutral route). Additionally on the test sessions, participants climbed the three routes in three different instruction conditions: a free condition (to observe the spontaneous behavior), an alternation condition (i.e., they were invited to perform as much alternations as they could on the routes) and a repetition condition (i.e., they were invited to perform as much repetitions as they could). Then, on the training sessions, participants climbed on more sophisticated routes where they were instructed to use all the handholds in a bottom-up order and to climb as fluently as possible, that is, avoiding saccades and stops during the ascents. That way, they had to search for the most adapted chain of movements for the route. According to their training group, participants climbed one to ten different routes during the training sessions. All groups had one route in common that they climbed at least three times per session (i.e., the Control route). Finally, the training protocol started (i.e., first ascent of the first training session) and ended (i.e., last ascent of the tenth training session) with one trial on a Transfer route for which they had no additional practice during the training sessions. This route was designed to assess whether the participants were able to find adapted chain of movements on new routes with training.

In many cases we dispose large registered data sets that can be labelled manually based on observations. Therefore in the whole process human mistakes in the labeling and the presence of artifacts in the recordings are inevitable - both error sources can prompt missing values in the labeling sequences. We would like to use the subset of partially labeled observations (recording of handhold touch time combined with the mass centre position, see Fig. 1 (b)) to predict the labeling (i.e left or right, hand or foot) of the whole dataset. As the data set consists of the pair sequences (observations and *incomplete* labels), thus we will apply the sequential learning with hidden Markov model. The challenging part is to manage the missing parts of the sequences and learn from the annotated parts to fill up the gaps with constrained Viterbi algorithm. Our task is similar to entity recognition with the average labeling ratio about one third of the sequence.

Fig. 2. The protocol of data collection with session profile (number of ascends in each session is provided in the box). The PREtest, POSTtest and RETention sessions (yellow) stand for the partially labeled sequences in our training dataset. They consist of simple routes (Neutral, Alternation and Repetition type); Transfer route opens and closes the Training Session. Each of the 10 Training Sessions (the unannotated data set, for which we predict the labels with our model) starts with the Control Route.

4 Methods

4.1 HMM Viterbi Training on Fully Labeled Sequences

The sequential learning task [8] is to find the relation between the observation sequence $o = (o_1, o_2, ..., o_T)$ and its pair label sequence $l = (l_1, l_2, ..., l_T)$, where each $l_t \in \{L_1, L_2, ..., L_n\} = L$ (assuming the sequences o are some continuous trains of measurements of length T and labels are the limbs: LH, RH, LF, RF). For HMM supervised learning framework [17], with fully labeled pairs (o, l), this relationship is described with a generative model m. It is subsequently applied, with the use of Viterbi algorithm [20], on new sequences of observations in order to find most likely corresponding label sequences (Fig. 3(a)). We notify, that by applying the Viterbi algorithm we obtain *hard* label assignation, whereas by using Baum-Welsh algorithm we would get probabilistic one. The former hard assignation is necessary for the next step of the processing in sport science: climb profiling by clustering (not presented here). Seemingly, there is a relation within each pair (o_t, l_t) all along the sequences, which we describe with probability of observation emission $e_s(o_t) = P(o_t|l_t = s)$. In case of a Markov process, there is no dependence between non-adjacent labels, whereas, there is one between the adjacent labels in the sequence l, that is described with the probability of transition $f_{rs} = P(l_{t+1} = r|l_t = s)$. Both mentioned types of conditional probabilities, that in case of sequences apply to every element of sequences o and l, in form of matrices $E = (e_s(o_t))_{s \in L, 1 \le t \le T}$ and $F = (f_{rs})_{r,s \in L}$, as well as initial probabilities $p_s = P(l_1 = s)$, adjusted to data pairs (o, l) are the parameters of our model $m = (p, E, F)$. We find the optimal parameters by maximizing the joint probability $P(o, l)$. Once the model parameters are found, we predict new labels for unlabeled observations o with Viterbi algorithm. The algorithm, starting from p and propagating through the observation sequence o, stores the probabilities of most likely path of labels l that generated o and same time, the most likely label sequence. The resulting optimal $\hat{l}$ is the sequence of argmax, once we have found all the probabilities. At first, in the framework of hidden Markov model, we calculate the joint probability for the sequence of observations o and the sequence of labels l as

$$P(o,l) = p_s \prod_{t=1}^{T} P(o_t|l_t) \prod_{t=1}^{T-1} P(l_{t+1}|l_t) \tag{1}$$

and we estimate the parameters of model m by maximizing log-likelihood

$$\hat{m} = \arg\max_{m} \sum_{i=1}^{n} \log P(o,l|m). \tag{2}$$

Subsequently, with the Viterbi algorithm, the parameters, in a recursive manner and through T steps, serve to compute the maximum-likelihood label sequence $\hat{l}$ given the observation sequence o.

The recurrence is used to track the v and w intermittent variables:

$$v_{0,s} = p_s \tag{3}$$

$$v_{t,s} = \max_{r} v_{t-1,r} f_{rs} e_s(o_t) \tag{4}$$

$$w_{t,s} = \arg\max_{r} v_{t-1,r} f_{rs} \tag{5}$$

and that for the last estimate label element

$$\hat{l}_T = \arg\max_{r} v_{T,r} \tag{6}$$

by backtracking we find the whole estimate sequence

$$\hat{l}_t = w_{t+1,\hat{l}_{t+1}}. \tag{7}$$

Thus, the ultimate sequence $\hat{l}$ is the optimal sequence of labels. The optimality of the Viterbi algorithm can be shown as in [16].

4.2   Our Contribution: HMM Viterbi Training on Partially Labeled Sequences

In case of partially labeled sequences in training set, we must adapt the basic supervised HMM procedure in order to train only from the labeled chunks of the sequences. For this purpose we will use the constrained Viterbi algorithm [4,9]. Firstly, we can notify that for unsupervised learning (when all the observations are unlabeled), we can randomly initialize the model parameters m and use the Expectation-Maximization algorithm to find both the m and the sequence of labels in fully unsupervised framework. The herewith technique combines the supervised and unsupervised learning so that initially and in each EM iteration, we take advantage of the labeled chunks of the sequences and constrain the unsupervised scenario.

Namely, we initialize the model with random parameters or with pre-training held on only labeled chunks of the sequences (l_t, o_t), for which we get interim

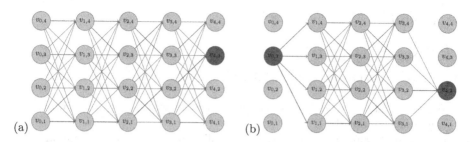

Fig. 3. (a) Standard Viterbi algorithm. The magenta path is the optimal one, ending with the maximum v value (magenta circle). All the possible paths (in cyan) are explored. At each tracking/forward step the most likely path to each state is recorded (dark magenta). At the end, only the path that leads to the most likely ending state is retained (magenta). (b) Constrained Viterbi algorithm. Here, only the paths that contain the first and last pre-fixed states are explored during the forward stage.

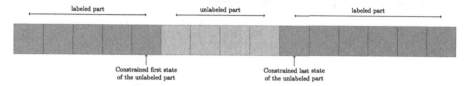

Fig. 4. Example of partially annotated sequence. Constrained Viterbi is applied on blue chunk accounting for the last magenta token of the first labelled chunk and first magenta token of the second labelled chunk.

parameters $\hat{m}$. In the next step, we find the interim labels $\hat{l}$ for the partially labeled sequence (Fig. 4) with the use of constrained Viterbi, that is enforced to move through the already known label chunks, by maximizing the probability of the most likely label path. Indeed, in the constrained scheme, the traditional Viterbi algorithm operates on the unlabeled segments of sequences, but with the first and the last states labeled (which are the fixed adjacent tokens), treating each chunk sequence independently (Fig. 3(b)). Subsequently, we use the fully labeled sequences $\hat{l}$ to generate new model parameters $\hat{m}$ and further adjust the labeling on the initially unlabeled parts of the sequences. While EM finds the local optimum, we iterate until convergence to find the best representation in terms of log-likelihood of the label sequence joint probability (Algorithm 1).

Algorithm 1. HMM with constrained Viterbi

1: *Initialization*: train model $\hat{m}$ with *only* fully labeled chunks of sequences (o, l)
2: **repeat**
3:     *Step 1 (E)*: complete the gaps in the sequences of labels with constrained Viterbi
    algorithm (parameters calculated with model $\hat{m}$), to get fully labeled estimates $(o, \hat{l})$
4:     *Step 2 (M)*: update model $\hat{m}$ due to new labels $(o, \hat{l})$
5: **until** *End condition*: iteration number

5 Results

5.1 Experimental Setting

We test the model on the following data:

1. synthetic data set from known model parameters where some annotations are randomly discarded,
2. experimental climbing data - chunks of full sequences with some annotations randomly discarded,
3. experimental climbing data - original partially labelled sequences.

For the synthetic data generation we used the Gaussian bi-variate distribution for the four label states. All the four states have the same covariance $\mathbf{S}$, they differ on their mean $\mathbf{m}$. For each of the two dimension of the mean, we used either $-\mu$ or μ, leading to 4 possibles states as shown in Eq. 8:

$$\mathbf{m}_1 = \begin{pmatrix} \mu \\ \mu \end{pmatrix} \quad , \quad \mathbf{m}_2 = \begin{pmatrix} \mu \\ -\mu \end{pmatrix} \quad , \quad \mathbf{m}_3 = \begin{pmatrix} -\mu \\ \mu \end{pmatrix} \quad , \quad \mathbf{m}_4 = \begin{pmatrix} -\mu \\ -\mu \end{pmatrix} \quad , \quad \mathbf{S} = \sigma\mathbf{I}. \tag{8}$$

So defined synthetic data distribution was to approximate the statistics of the climbing data. To apply random label discarding in fully labeled sequences, the level of gap ratio has been fixed (0.25). For the experimental sport data set (points 2 and 3), we dispose the 497 partially annotated sequences of observations (simple sessions), which are divided into train and test sets. The labeling with four types of limbs, reaches the annotation level of about 0.3 for the sequences of the average length of 20 tokens. Finally, the established model will be used for the annotation of overall number of about 3700 sequences recorded with touch sensors. In order to evaluate model performance in case of the first two data sets (where ground true labeling has been initially known), we calculated accuracy measure which is similarity ratio (averaged sum over whole sequence, scoring 0 for mismatch and 1 for match on each token in the sequence) employed on the fully labeled initial sequence l (before label removal) vs the sequence estimated by the model $\hat{l}$. Hence, the evaluation score for a whole sequence l and its prediction $\hat{l}$ reads

$$d(l, \hat{l}) = \frac{1}{T} \sum_{t=1}^{T} d_t(l_t, \hat{l}_t) \tag{9}$$

with the loss function d_t defined over two tokens l_t and $\hat{l}_t$ as

$$d_t(l_t, \hat{l}_t) = \begin{cases} 1 & \text{for } l_t = \hat{l}_t, \\ 0 & \text{otherwise.} \end{cases} \tag{10}$$

To test the hidden Markov model with constrained Viterbi we used synthetically generated data with known parameters. The missing labels was to best resemble the true annotation present in real data (the gap ratio of about 0.3).

We compared the predicted model parameters with the original counterpart as well as the scoring in two sequences: label sequence generated with original model and label sequence estimated with predicted model parameters. The same way of evaluation has been employed for experimental data with full annotations. In these cases we are able to compare the resulting fully labelled sequences with the initial true labels, before label removal. For all the dataset however, the likelihood of the observation sequences knowing the model parameters is always accessible whether the true labels are fully known, partially known or totally unknown. To sum-up, in case of fully labelled sequences altered artificially to partially labelled ones (dataset 1 and 2), we can compute a similarity ratio comparing the estimated labels to the true ones. Otherwise (dataset 3), only the likelihood of the HMM is accessible as an evaluation measure.

5.2   Evaluation

Synthetic Data Set. As explained in point 1, firstly we have tested the model on artificially generated data (with either random initialization or pre-trained on labeled chunks of sequences). The number of sequences in trained and test sets was 1000, the average length of sequences was about 20 tokens, with label gap ratio equal to 0.25. We analyse the log-likelihood over the joint probability of observation and labeling sequences that evolves across the iterations for label distribution with mean 1.5 and covariance 0.2 (Fig. 5). This value determines how well the label sequence describes their pair observation sequence, based on the label distribution. As expected, we observe monotonic increase of log-likelihood over the iterations, as well as for the similarity score computed for unannotated chunks. The stability is reached after 2nd iteration. The log-likelihood evolution proves that the model fits well with the experimental data and at the same time leads to the generation of optimal labels. Likewise, score analysis confirm increasing recognition of labels if compared to the ground true annotations in the subsequent steps.

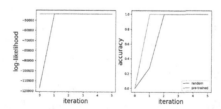

Fig. 5. Synthetic data set (generated with mean parameter $\mu = 1.5$ and covariance parameter $\sigma = 0.2$): log-likelihood value evolution (left) and similarity ratio (right). The labels have been discarded with ratio 0.25. The applied initialization was either random (blue) or pre-trained (orange) on the labeled chunks. (Color figure online)

Climbing Data Set. We first explore the real experimental dataset with artificial deletion of the annotations (with an alteration rate of 0.3). On the artificially deleted slots, we do have knowledge of the true labeling, thus we can compute the similarity ratio. After alternation, first, we pre-trained the HMM on the fully labeled chunks of sequences, bypassing the voids. Then, the HMM was trained using the constrained Viterbi in the manner exposed in the Methods 4, with all the partially labelled sequences. In the Fig. 6(a), we observe learning through iterations (growth of the log-likelihood), and at the same time - the annotations of the labels are mostly correct (the maximum similarity ratio is over 0.9).

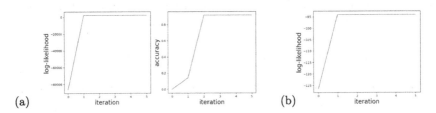

Fig. 6. Sport data set. (a) Sequences originally fully labeled but with artificial label deletion: log-likelihood evolution (left) and similarity ratio (right). In order to apply the model, the labels have been synthetically discarded with ratio of about 0.25. (b) original data, partially labeled with gap ratio about 0.3: log-likelihood evolution.

Based on this fact, we studied the case of partially labeled original sequences registered by touch sensors (Point 3). Similarly, for experimental sport data we observe monotonic growth of the log-probability function, which is - as in synthetic data case and the artificially discarded labelings in sport data - depicting learning across the iterations. While the ratio of unannotated labels in all three experimental data cases was about 0.3, we may expect that the results are comparable. Like in the previous data sets, in the original partially labeled sport data, the model log-likelihood converges also very fast, within two iterations (Fig. 6(b)). In this case, unlike the previous two cases, since the true labels remain unknown, the similarity ratio is not accessible. The end-values of log-likelihood function however, are lower than in the artificially label discarded sport data case. We may suppose that this fact could have an impact on the quality of the label prediction. Although we do not dispose any other objective evaluation method, the convergence of the model may be a proof of leading towards the correct solution. We assume that the mislabelling, if applicable, might have occurred in case the artifacts appear in the collected data (e.g. when the sensor registered a touch made not by the hand or foot).

To complete the analysis, we pursued the machine learning evaluation method in which for synthetic data train set to test set ratio was 1000:1000 and for the sport data annotated sequences we split the data set with the ratio 400:97. Namely, we verified the accuracy of the model trained on one subset of partially labeled data (train set), when applied on the previously unused subset of data with no labeling (test set). For this setting, the similarity score evaluated on the new test sequences were not substantially different from the previously observed training evaluation (Table 1), and confirmed correct label attribution.

Table 1. Similarity score for synthetic data set vs climbing data set.

Data set	Training	Testing
Synthetic	0.99	0.99
Climbing	0.91	0.90

6 Conclusion and Perspective

In the present article, we have been studying how the generative model (HMM) with a simple adjustment (constrained Viterbi) deals with the learning the partial labelling in the training sequences. It is a predictive model, that allows to access the distribution of the limbs used while climbing the artificial wall. We tested the approach on the real climbing data as well as on the synthetic data, that was alike. We claim that, based on the log-likelihood value, which specifies how good is the description that we find for the measured data, due to our experiments we can judge on model performance. We must admit however, that the additional challenge we face in our application is the discrete set of states (labels). This situation renders difficult to measure the effective labelling ratio based only on log-likelihood value. We have compared the log-likelihood ratio with similarity score computed for unannotated chunks in cases, when the full labelling has been known in order to assert patterns of likelihood function. We observed that it proves apt attribution of labels in case of the data set, when the prior full labelling is not accessible, as in the sport data set. We have demonstrated, that the log-likelihood matches scoring and can be used for model evaluation in case of training on only partially labeled data sets.

Perspective. We can show experimentally that the log-likelihood convergence with a general tendency of monotonic increase (and not decrease) approximates correct label attribution. In a broader setting though, HMM with constrained Viterbi may not be a perfect label predictor for the continuous behavioral signal, but is a simple way to approximate labelling of unknown sequence, with scarce prior knowledge about training sample. Therefore, to outperform our algorithm, some more sophisticated method, as for instance neural networks would have to be applied. Likewise, the convergence of optimality function for the leading model (not only for the Viterbi constrained, but its implementation into the framework of EM-like full Algorithm 1), requires more systematic research and theoretically correct proof. Although the model is simplistic and its output may not be faultless, it is still sufficient for the first approximation of the behavioral signal labelling in sport application and it can be the baseline for the further research on the subject, that could be tested in the contexts of different paradigms in human movement science.

Acknowledgement. This work was supported by a grant from the French National Agency of Research (reference: ANR-17-CE38-0006 DynACEV).

References

1. Antoniuk, V., Franc, V., Hlavac, V.: Consistency of structured output learning with missing labels. In: Holmes, G., Liu, T.Y. (eds.) JMLR: Workshop and Conference Proceedings, pp. 81–95. ACML 2015 (2015)
2. Blum, A., Mitchell, T.: Combining labeled andunlabeled data with co-training. In: Proceedings of the Workshop on Computational Learning Theory. pp. 92–100 (1998)
3. Boulanger, J., Seifert, L., Hérault, R., Coeurjolly, J.F.: Automatic sensor-based detection and classification of climbing activities. IEE Sensors J. **16**(3), 742–749 (2016)
4. Cao, L., Chen, C.W.: A novel product coding and recurrent alternate decoding scheme for image transmission over noisy channels. IEEE Trans. Commun. **51**, 1426–1431 (2003)
5. Chapelle, O., Scholkopf, B., Zien, A.: Semi-supervised Learning. MIT Press, Cambridge (2006)
6. Clark, K., Luong, M.T., Manning, C., Le, Q.: Semi-supervised sequence modeling with cross-view training. In: Proceedings of the 2018 Conference on Empirical Methods in Natural Language Processing. pp. 1914–1925. Association for Computational Linguistics, Brussels, Belgium (2018). https://www.aclweb.org/anthology/D18-1217
7. Dai, A., Le, Q.: Semi-supervised sequence learning. In: Proceedings of Neural Information Processing Systems Conference. pp. 1–10 (2015)
8. Dietterich, T.: Machine learning for sequential data: a review. In: Proceedings of the Joint IAPR International Workshop on Structural, Syntactic, and Statistical Pattern Recognition. vol. 1, pp. 1–15 (2002)
9. Fernandes, E., Brefeld, U.: Learning from Partially Annotated Sequences. Springer-Verlag, Berlin (2011)
10. Fernandes, E., Brefeld, U., Blanco, R., Atserias, J.: Using Wikipedia for cross-language named entity recognition. In: Atzmueller, M., Chin, A., Janssen, F., Schweizer, I., Trattner, C. (eds.) Big Data Analytics in the Social and Ubiquitous Context, pp. 1–25. Springer International Publishing, Cham (2016)
11. Hacques, G., Komar, J., Bourbousson, J., Seifert, L.: Climbers' learning dynamics: an exploratory study. In: 4th International Rock Climbing Congress (IRCRA). Chamonix, France, 12–15th July (2018)
12. Huang, X., Dong, L., Boschee, E., Peng, N.: Learning a unified named entity tagger from multiple partially annotated corpora for efficient adaptation. In: Proceedings of the 23rd Conference on Computational Natural Language Learning. pp. 515–527 (2019)
13. Li, J., Liu, C., Liu, B.: Large scale sequential learning from partially labeled data. In: 2013 IEEE Seventh International Conference on Semantic Computing. pp. 176–183 (2013)
14. Mikolov, T., Sutskever, I., Chen, K., Corrado, G., Dean, J.: Distributed representations of words and phrases and their compositionality. In: NIPS (2013)
15. Ning, Q., He, H., Fan, C., Roth, D.: Partial or complete, that's the question. In: Proceedings of NAACL Conference. pp. 2190–2200 (2019). https://doi.org/10.18653/v1/N19-1227

16. Omura, J.: On the Viterbi decoding algorithm. IEEE Trans. Inf. Theory **15**(1), 177–179 (1969)
17. Rabiner, R.: A tutorial on hidden Markov models and selected applications on speech recognition. Proc. IEEE **77**(2), 257–286 (1989)
18. Scheffer, T., Decomain, C., Wrobel, S.: Active hidden Markov models for information extraction. In: Proceedings of the 4th International Conference on Advances in Intelligent Data Analysis. pp. 309–318 (2001)
19. Veeramachaneni, W., Liao, V.: A simple semi-supervised algorithm for named entity recognition. In: Workshop on Semi-supervised Learning for Natural Language Processing pp. 58–65 (2009)
20. Viterbi, A.: Error bounds for convolutional codes and an asymptotically optimum decoding algorithm. IEEE Trans. Inf. Theory **13**(2), 260–269 (1967). https://doi.org/10.1109/TIT.1967.1054010
21. Zhi, S., Liu, L., Zhang, Y., Wang, S., Li, Q., Zhang, C., Han, J.: Partially-typed NER datasets integration: Connecting practice to theory. (in press) pp. 1–13 (2020)
22. Zhou, J., et al.: Learning with annotation of various degrees. IEEE Trans. Neural Networks Learn. Syst. **30**(9), 2794–2804 (2019). https://doi.org/10.1109/TNNLS.2018.2885854

Author Index

Printed in the United States
By Bookmasters